THE M5 ANTI-BOREDOM GUIDE

Richard Shurey

THORNHILL PRESS
CHELTENHAM

C Richard Shurey, 1985

ISBN 0 946328 11 0

Printed by
STOATE & BISHOP (PRINTERS) LIMITED
CHELTENHAM & GLOUCESTER

THE M5 ANTI-BOREDOM GUIDE

To be encased as a passenger in a little tin box for several hours on a motorway can be the most boring of experiences. But as one gazes out at the landscape flashing past, the questions are inevitably posed - where is that lovely cathedral on the horizon? What is the airfield? And that strange folly on a hilltop - why was that built? Those cranes on a distant estuary - where are they? Is that a Norman church in the little village? And so on . . . .

The purpose of this book is to try to convince you that a journey along the M5 is to travel along a most interesting motorway.

Before we set out let us consider a few thoughts on how the modern road system evolved in Britain. The motorways have been likened to the Roman highways.

The skilled planned network left to us by the Roman invaders were superimposed on a landscape where the tracks (often made by animals wandering over sure dry ground) were haphazard and merely used to link single communities.

The Roman highways served the country well - practically no further planned roads were constructed until the 17th century. Hilaire Belloc told us that "they account for the site of most battles, of most great monasteries, of most marts, of most palaces; for the development of all campaigns".

Whilst many continental countries obliterated their Roman roads, England kept hers almost intact - apart from the "poaching" of stones for the construction of buildings! Other routes - the ancient "Green Roads"- had no proper surface and were pot-holed and hazardous. The road engineers of the 18th century up-graded the old ways into modern highways which adequately served the carriage trade. With the arrival of the new motor vehicles around the turn of the century the inadequacy of the road system was soon apparent. Little was done to make new roads. There were hesitant steps after the first World War with a few "arterial" highways.

Belloc argued the merits of "motorways" - direct routes - from which horses and pedestrians were excluded and which would incorporate bridges or tunnels to accommodate crossing traffic. As an example he considered a London to Birmingham road which closely resembled the subsequent route and shape of the motorway.

However, it was the Germans who demonstrated the economic and strategic benefits of new inter-city routes with the start of the autobahn programme in 1928. Between 1933 and 1945, 2100 km of motorways were built. Britain waited until 1957 for her first motorway - the Preston by-pass, now part of the M6.

So, while the driver concentrates on the road, it is eyes peeled for the passengers to spot the many intriguing features near the M5. The distances shown are approximate from the centre of each junction. Each page covers about 2½ miles and can be used on journeys South to North or North to South or between any intervening junctions.

Bon Voyage!   Richard Shurey

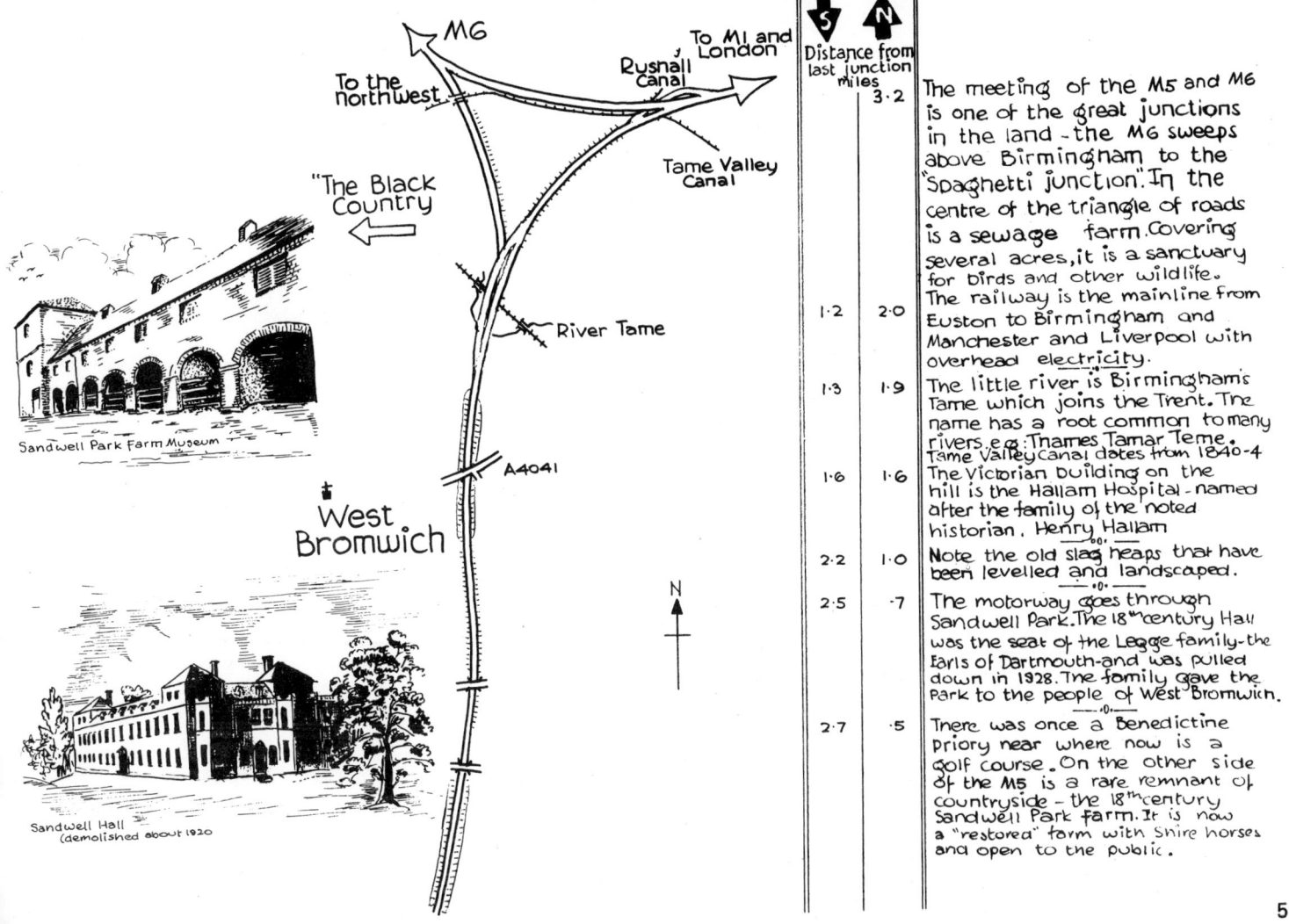

Distance from last junction miles S	N	
	3.2	The meeting of the M5 and M6 is one of the great junctions in the land - the M6 sweeps above Birmingham to the "Spaghetti junction". In the centre of the triangle of roads is a sewage farm. Covering several acres, it is a sanctuary for birds and other wildlife.
1.2	2.0	The railway is the mainline from Euston to Birmingham and Manchester and Liverpool with overhead electricity.
1.3	1.9	The little river is Birmingham's Tame which joins the Trent. The name has a root common to many rivers, e.g. Thames Tamar Teme. Tame Valley Canal dates from 1840-4
1.6	1.6	The Victorian building on the hill is the Hallam Hospital - named after the family of the noted historian, Henry Hallam
2.2	1.0	Note the old slag heaps that have been levelled and landscaped.
2.5	.7	The motorway goes through Sandwell Park. The 18th century Hall was the seat of the Legge family - the Earls of Dartmouth - and was pulled down in 1928. The family gave the Park to the people of West Bromwich.
2.7	.5	There was once a Benedictine priory near where now is a golf course. On the other side of the M5 is a rare remnant of countryside - the 18th century Sandwell Park farm. It is now a "restored" farm with shire horses and open to the public.

Sandwell Park Farm Museum

West Bromwich

Sandwell Hall (demolished about 1920)

5

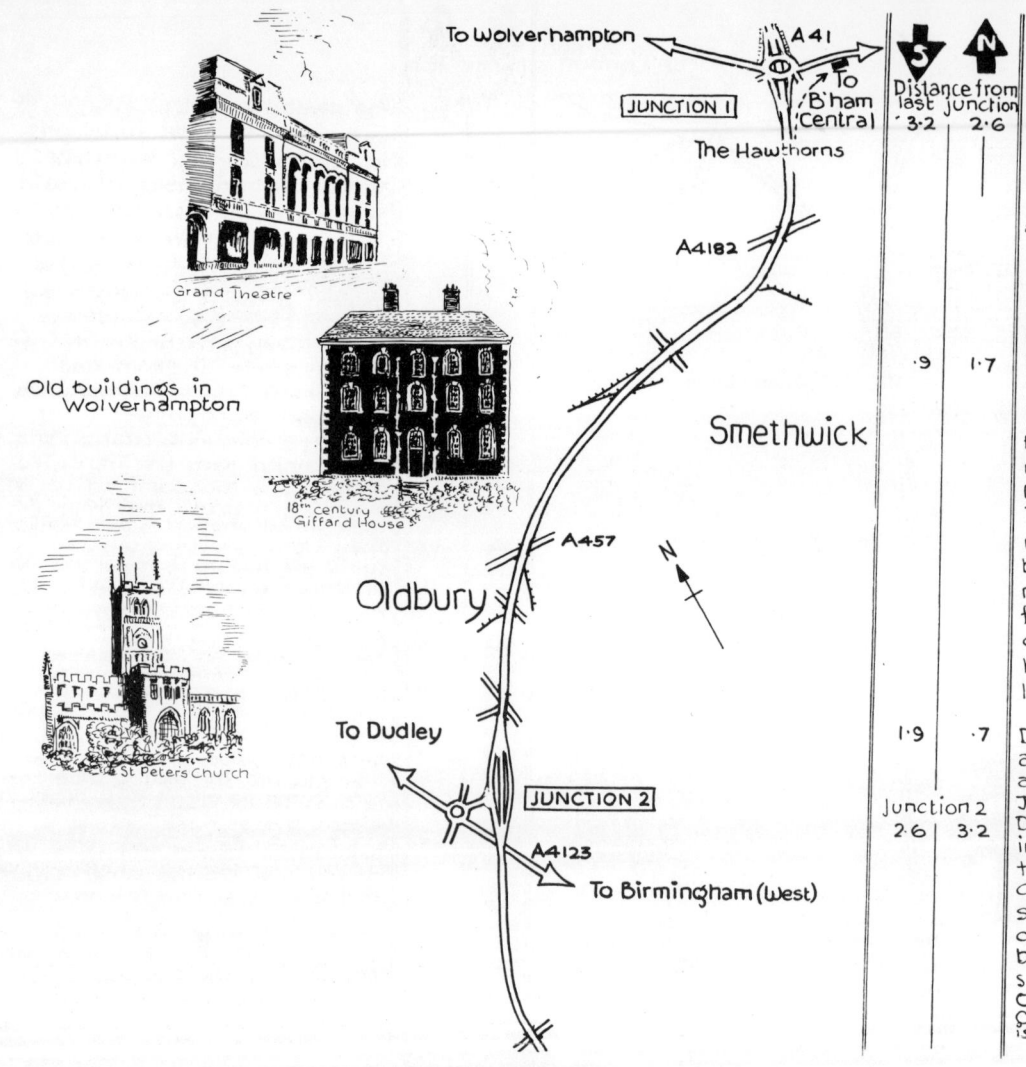

Distance from last junction	
S	N
3.2	2.6
.9	1.7
1.9	.7
Junction 2 2.6	3.2

The junction here is to Wolverhampton - the town grew rich on wool in the Middle Ages - the name is from Wulfram's High Town. In the 18th century iron came and the character of the town changed for ever. The church is medieval and magnificent. Alongside Junction 1 is "The Hawthorns" - the home of West Bromwich Albion Football Club. We pass above canals - part of Brindley's Birmingham Navigation. It dates from about 1772 - the tortuous route hugging contours was improved by Telford in 1824. We are now in the heart of The Black Country - the industry rapidly developed in the 19th c. because of the proximity of easily-mined coal, ironstone, limestone & fireclays. Now the old industries of steel, metal goods, springs etc have largely given way to light industry in small units.

Dudley Castle is on a hill 3 miles away - it was built in the 11th c. and was habitable until a fire (1750). Junction 2 - turn off to Dudley - some fascinating industrial museums and canal tunnels. A zoo is housed in the castle. The area around Dudley suffers from subsidence caused by old coal mines but the church with the spire has stood firm since 1817. On the Tipton Road is the Black Country Museum. On a 26 acre site is a colliery and old craft workshops

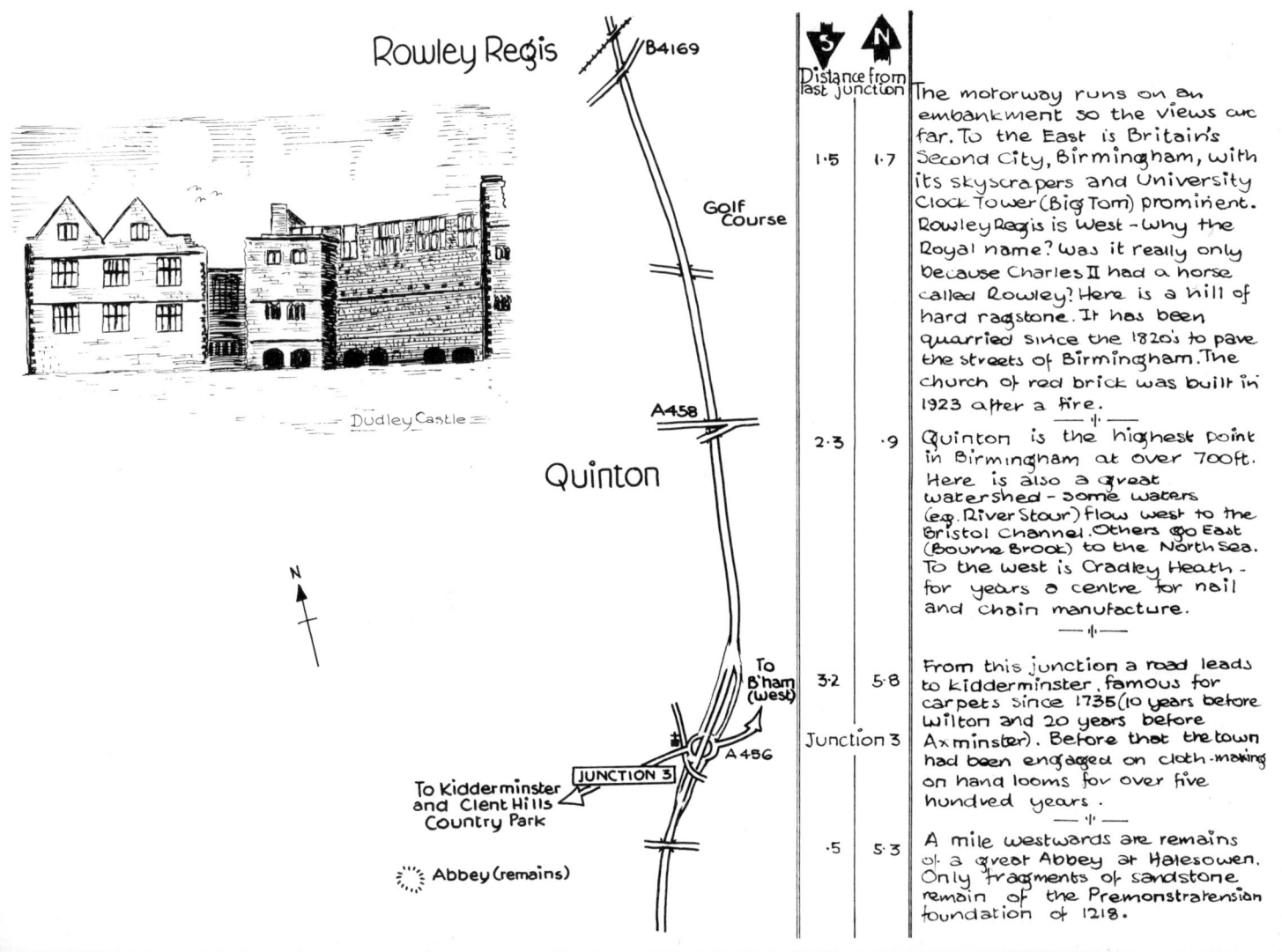

Distance from last junction		
1.5	1.7	The motorway runs on an embankment so the views are far. To the East is Britain's Second City, Birmingham, with its skyscrapers and University Clock Tower (Big Tom) prominent. Rowley Regis is West - why the Royal name? Was it really only because Charles II had a horse called Rowley? Here is a hill of hard ragstone. It has been quarried since the 1820's to pave the streets of Birmingham. The church of red brick was built in 1923 after a fire.
2.3	.9	Quinton is the highest point in Birmingham at over 700ft. Here is also a great watershed - some waters (eg. River Stour) flow west to the Bristol Channel. Others go East (Bourne Brook) to the North Sea. To the West is Cradley Heath - for years a centre for nail and chain manufacture.
3.2	5.8 Junction 3	From this junction a road leads to Kidderminster, famous for carpets since 1735 (10 years before Wilton and 20 years before Axminster). Before that the town had been engaged on cloth-making on hand looms for over five hundred years.
.5	5.3	A mile westwards are remains of a great Abbey at Halesowen. Only fragments of sandstone remain of the Premonstratensian foundation of 1218.

7

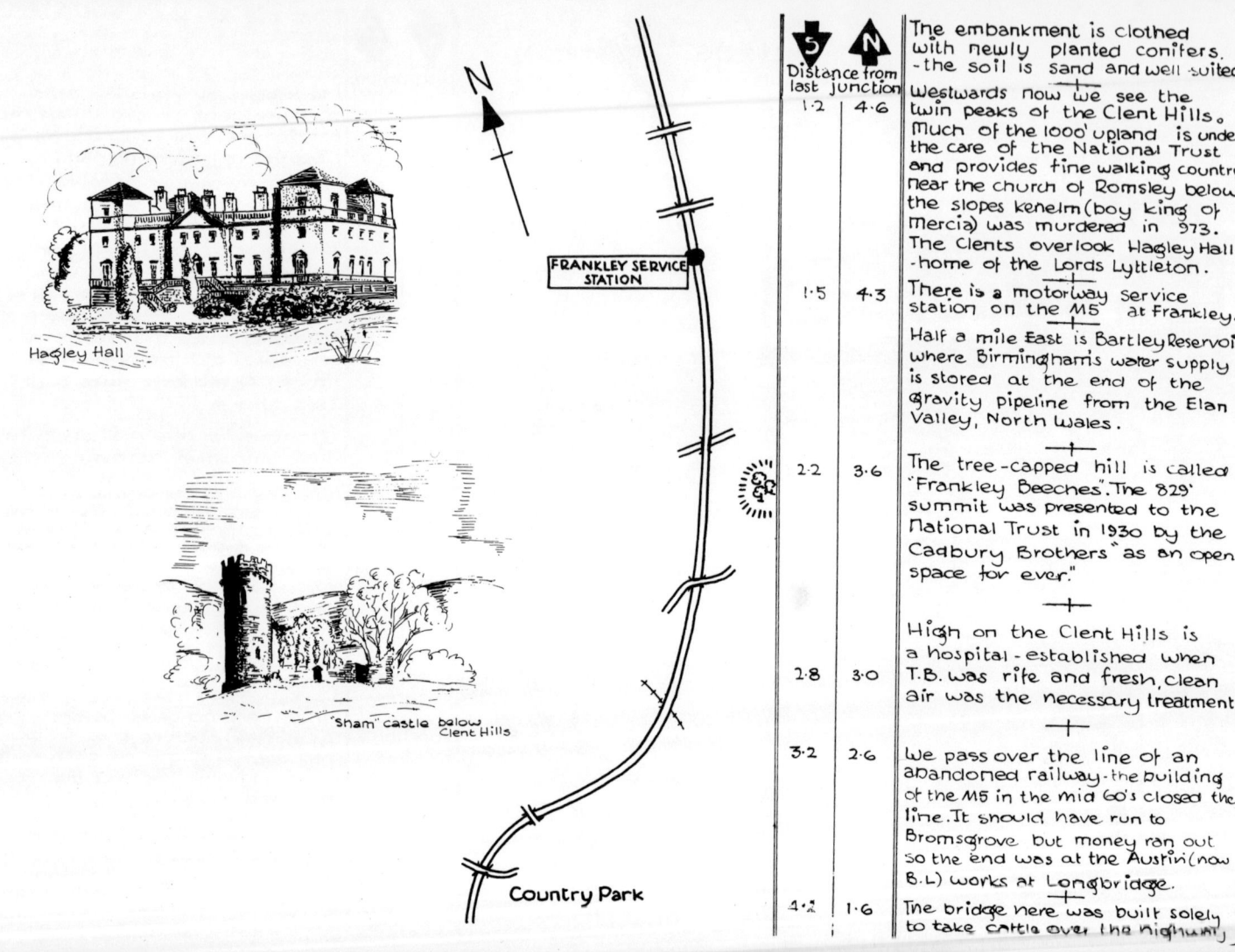

Hagley Hall

"Sham" castle below Clent Hills

Country Park

S Distance from last junction	N	
1.2	4.6	The embankment is clothed with newly planted conifers. -the soil is sand and well suited. Westwards now we see the twin peaks of the Clent Hills. Much of the 1000' upland is under the care of the National Trust and provides fine walking country. Near the church of Romsley below the slopes Kenelm (boy King of Mercia) was murdered in 973. The Clents overlook Hagley Hall -home of the Lords Lyttleton.
1.5	4.3	There is a motorway service station on the M5 at Frankley. Half a mile East is Bartley Reservoir where Birmingham's water supply is stored at the end of the gravity pipeline from the Elan Valley, North Wales.
2.2	3.6	The tree-capped hill is called "Frankley Beeches". The 829' summit was presented to the National Trust in 1930 by the Cadbury Brothers "as an open space for ever."
2.8	3.0	High on the Clent Hills is a hospital - established when T.B. was rife and fresh, clean air was the necessary treatment.
3.2	2.6	We pass over the line of an abandoned railway - the building of the M5 in the mid 60's closed the line. It should have run to Bromsgrove but money ran out so the end was at the Austin (now B.L) works at Longbridge.
4.2	1.6	The bridge here was built solely to take cattle over the highway.

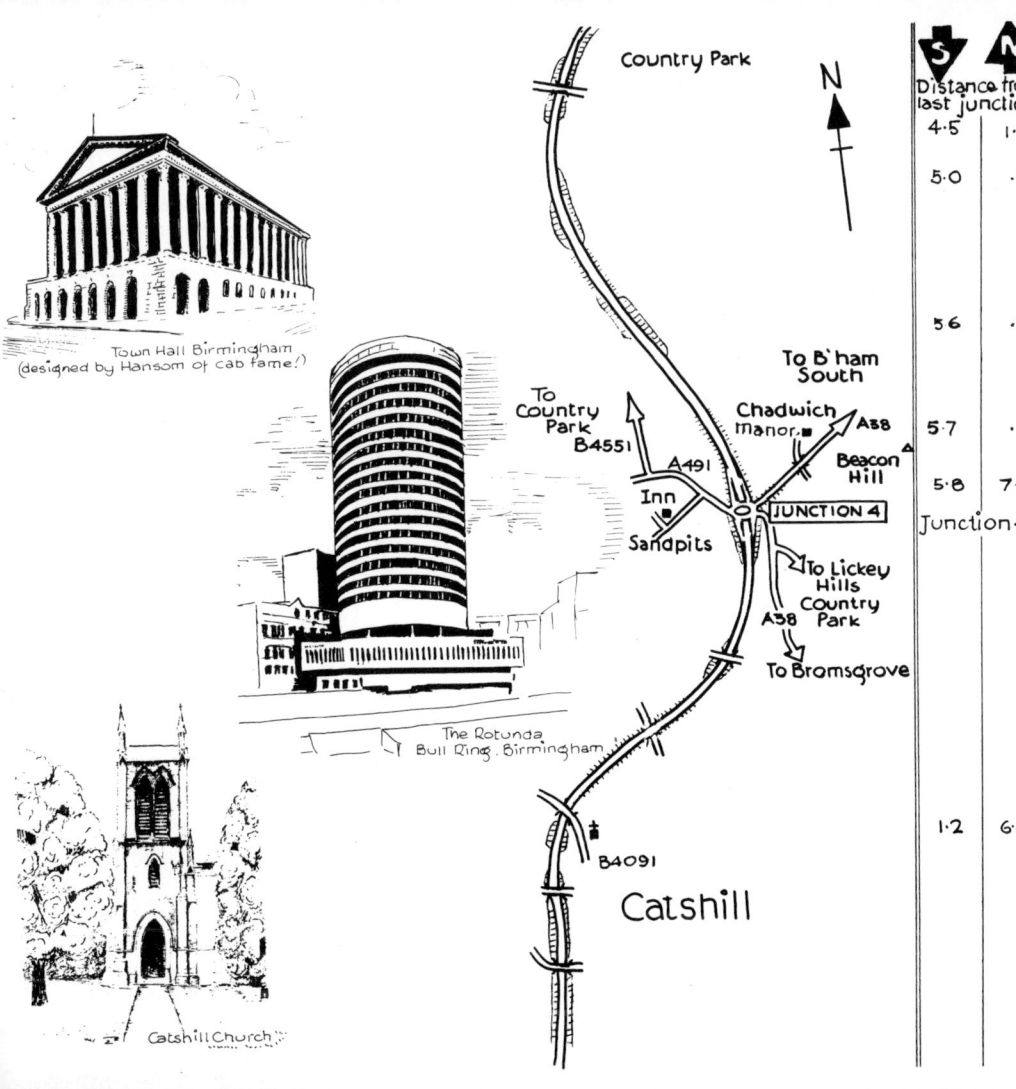

Distance from last junction S	N
4.5	1.3
5.0	.8
5.6	.2
5.7	.1
5.8 Junction 4	7.6
1.2	6.4

The hill to the West is Windmill Hill. The mill has long gone and this breezy place is where to fly kites — it is part of a large Country Park — these Parks were established under the powers granted by Parliament in 1949.

―――

The sandpits here are of red moulding sand. Its 20% felspar composition makes it especially suitable for small castings and non-ferrous (brass) foundings.

―――

The highest point on the Lickey Ridge is Beacon Hill (987') — an ancient signalling point used to spread the news of the approach of the Spanish Armada.

―――

Chadwich Manor is a fine red brick house dating from 1706.

―――

Junction 4 — an exit for the 800acre Lickey Hills Country Park. This is one of the main 'playgrounds' for Birmingham. The origins resulted from the 1803 Enclosure Act which threatened to restrict access to the Commons. Public spirited bodies purchased land for open use. Further acres were donated by the philanthropic Cadbury family. When the Birmingham Corporation took over and bought more land it was the first council in the country to acquire a nature reserve.

―――

Catshill is an insignificant village except for the fact that the first vicar of the new church in the last century was the grandfather of A.E. Housman, the celebrated poet.

―――

These are market garden areas to supply Birmingham with vegetables.

―――

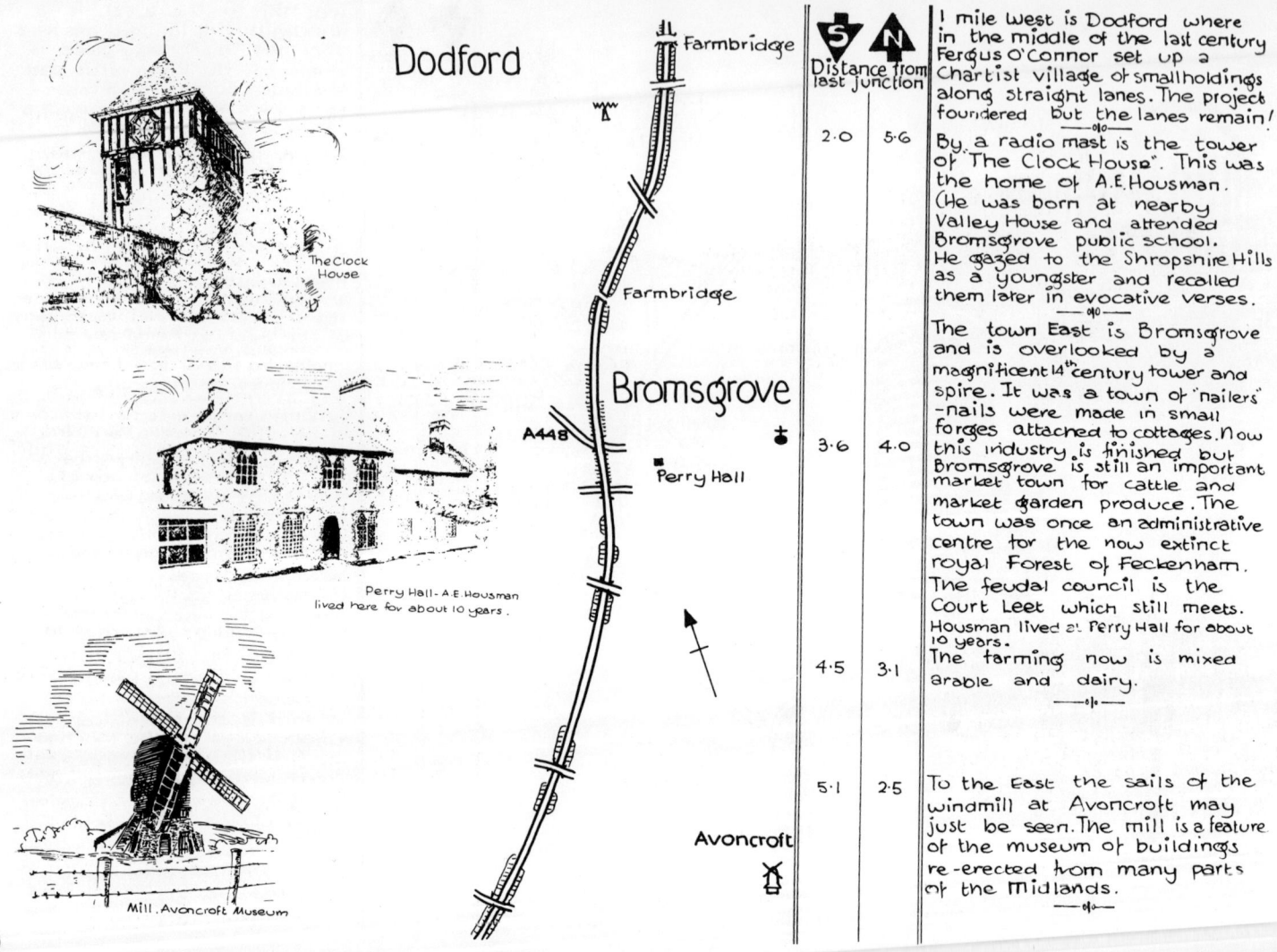

Distance from last junction	
S	N
2.0	5.6
3.6	4.0
4.5	3.1
5.1	2.5

1 mile West is Dodford where in the middle of the last century Fergus O'Connor set up a Chartist village of smallholdings along straight lanes. The project foundered but the lanes remain!

By a radio mast is the tower of "The Clock House". This was the home of A.E. Housman. (He was born at nearby Valley House and attended Bromsgrove public school. He gazed to the Shropshire Hills as a youngster and recalled them later in evocative verses.

The town East is Bromsgrove and is overlooked by a magnificent 14th century tower and spire. It was a town of "nailers" — nails were made in small forges attached to cottages. Now this industry is finished but Bromsgrove is still an important market town for cattle and market garden produce. The town was once an administrative centre for the now extinct royal Forest of Feckenham. The feudal council is the Court Leet which still meets. Housman lived at Perry Hall for about 10 years. The farming now is mixed arable and dairy.

To the East the sails of the windmill at Avoncroft may just be seen. The mill is a feature of the museum of buildings re-erected from many parts of the Midlands.

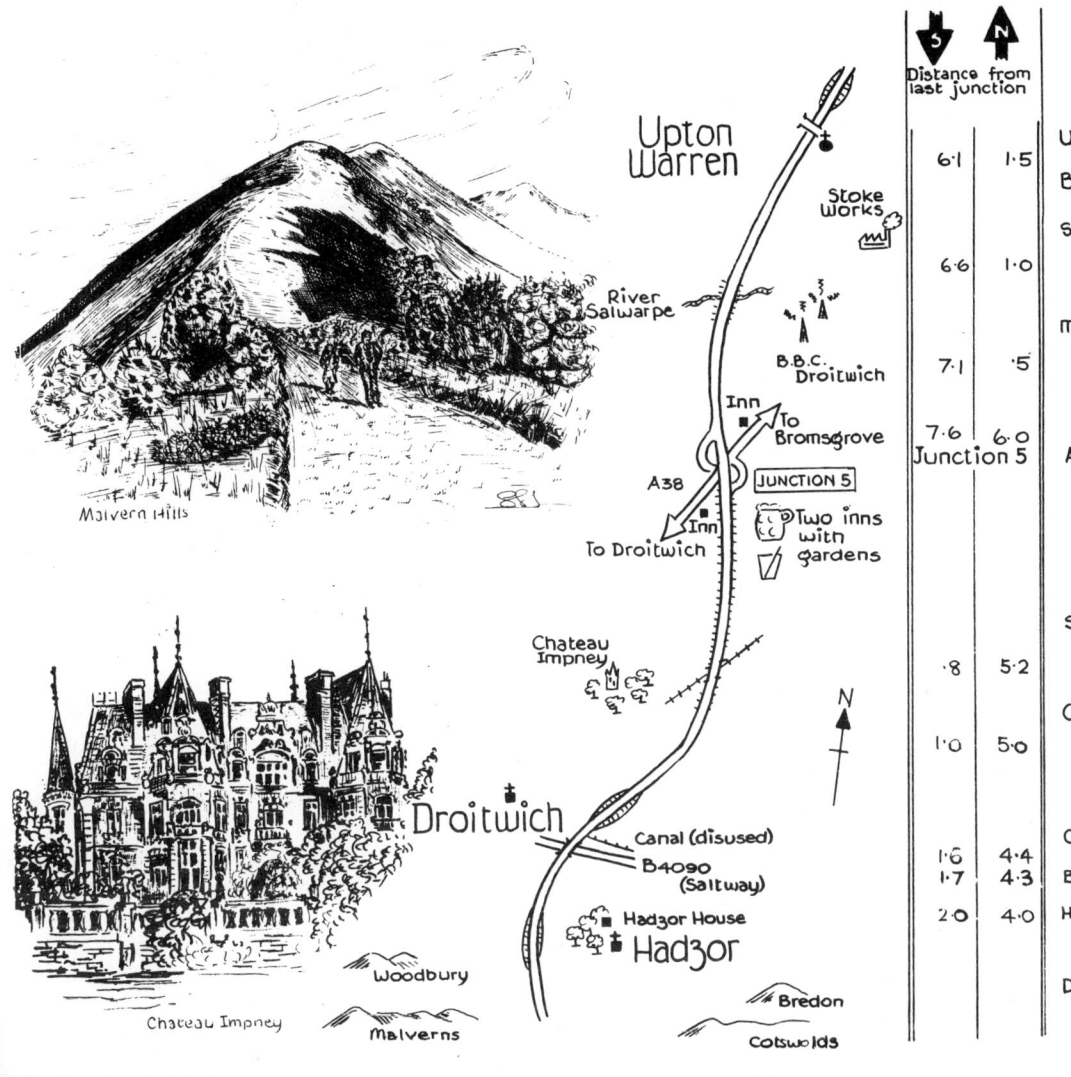

Distance from last junction (S)	(N)	
6.1	1.5	Upton Church - mostly 18th century - tower is 13th century. Bridge - note rollers underneath to allow for heat expansion.
6.6	1.0	Stoke Works - founded by John Corbett in 1828 to produce salt - the River Salwarpe is the "river of salt" - flows into Severn.
7.1	.5	Masts transmit B.B.C. radio programmes on Radio 1, 2, 3, 4 and World Service. The main masts are 700ft high and a lift conveys engineers almost to the top. The smaller mast (350) is a 'reserve'.
7.6 Junction 5	6.0	A38 was a Roman Road from Droitwich. The salt in the ground made the town famous. In the last century the healing brine baths turned the town into a fashionable spa. To the Romans Droitwich was Salinae.
.8	5.2	Single track railway - a rare branch line that links Droitwich with the main Midlands to the South-west route.
1.0	5.0	Chateau Impney - the turretted house was built for an industrialist (1869) - John Corbett used an architect from Paris to please his French-born wife; the place is now an hotel.
1.6	4.4	Canal - connected Worcester Canal to River Severn - now overgrown.
1.7	4.3	B4090 was an important salt route.
2.0	4.0	Hadzor House is now a college. The nearby church was built in the 14th century.
		Distant Hills - Woodbury-capped by fort. Malverns - some of the oldest rocks in UK. Bredon - just under 1000'. Cotswolds - a long limestone ridge.

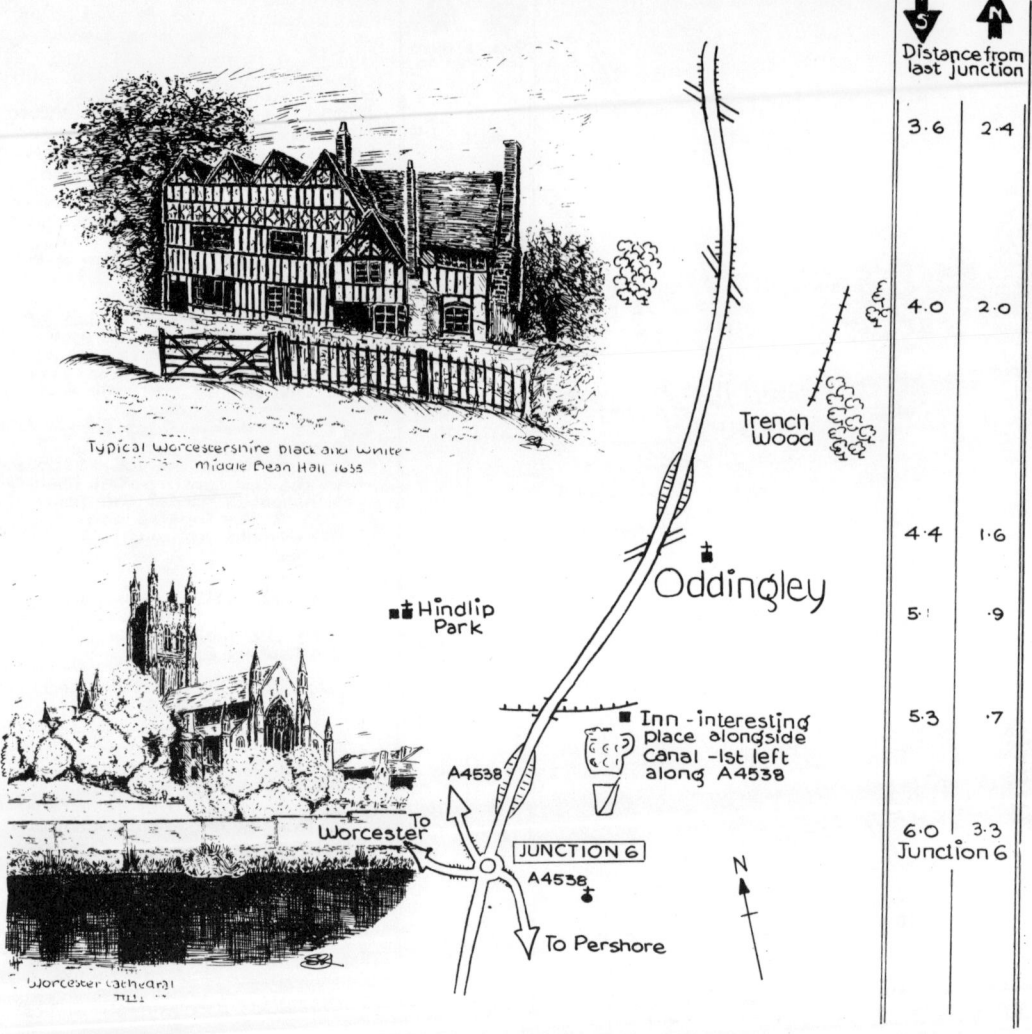

Typical Worcestershire black and white — Middle Bean Hall 1635

Worcester Cathedral

Distance from last junction		
S	N	
3.6	2.4	Feckenham Forest — Eastwards there are many pockets of old woods — the royal forest once stretched for some 30 miles but the saltworks needed vast quantities of timber for fuel and most of the trees were felled.
4.0	2.0	Railway — the main Midlands to South-West is not electrified and engines are diesel-electric.
		The motorway now near the River Severn — 4 miles to the west and stays in its valley for many miles.
4.4	1.6	Oddingley church — this isolated building has a 17th century tower.
5.1	.9	Hindlip Park — the house on this site was the home of John Habington, Queen Elizabeth I's treasurer. The present 19th c. building is a police H.q.
5.3	.7	Worcs. and Birmingham Canal — was completed in 1815 — the route connected Birmingham to the sea via the Severn but always suffered from shortage of water and never made money.
6.0 Junction 6	3.3	Worcester — there has been a settlement here for 2000 years. Romans called it Vertis. In the late Middle Ages cloth-making brought wealth. The cathedral building dates from 1041 but the splendid riverside site was used for an earlier church.
		Pershore — an Abbey town is in the Vale of Evesham and noted for orchards — leave motorway here for fruit!

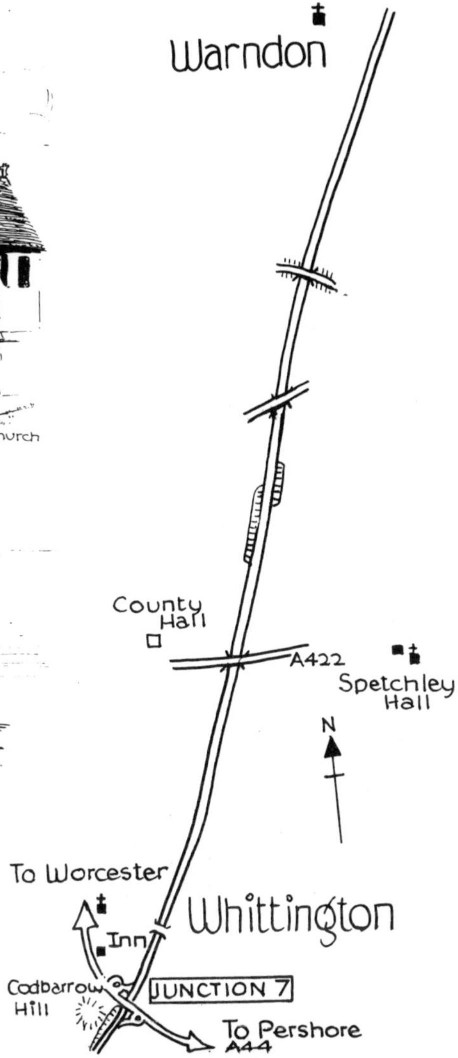

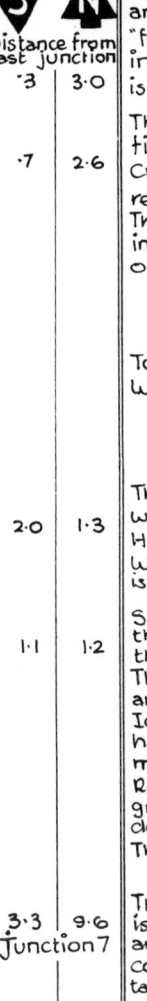

Distance from last junction S	N
.3	3.0
.7	2.6
2.0	1.3
1.1	1.2
3.3 Junction 7	9.6

Warndon Church is 13C; its black and white low tower is an ancient "forest church" (once in a clearing in the Forest of Feckenham). It is a classic 'unrestored' building.

—o—

The church across the fields two miles east is at Crowle - it was completely rebuilt in the last century. The Manor of Crowle was once in the possession of the priors of Worcester.

—o—

To the west is the City of Worcester.

The new County Hall (built with some controversy as H.Q. for the Herefordshire and Worcestershire County Council) is by the A422 at Nunnery Wood.

—o—

Spetchley has been the home of the Berkeley family for more than three hundred years. The house is in Regency style and built in 1810 with a fine Ionic portico. The previous house was occupied by Cromwell's men then subsequently the Royalists burnt the house to the ground. The name 'Spetchley' denotes 'speech place' in past days. The nearby church is 14th century.

The mound near the junction is Crookbarrow Hill. It was an ancient British camp. Roman coins have established it was taken over from the Celts.

—o—

Warndon Church

Spetchley Hall

13

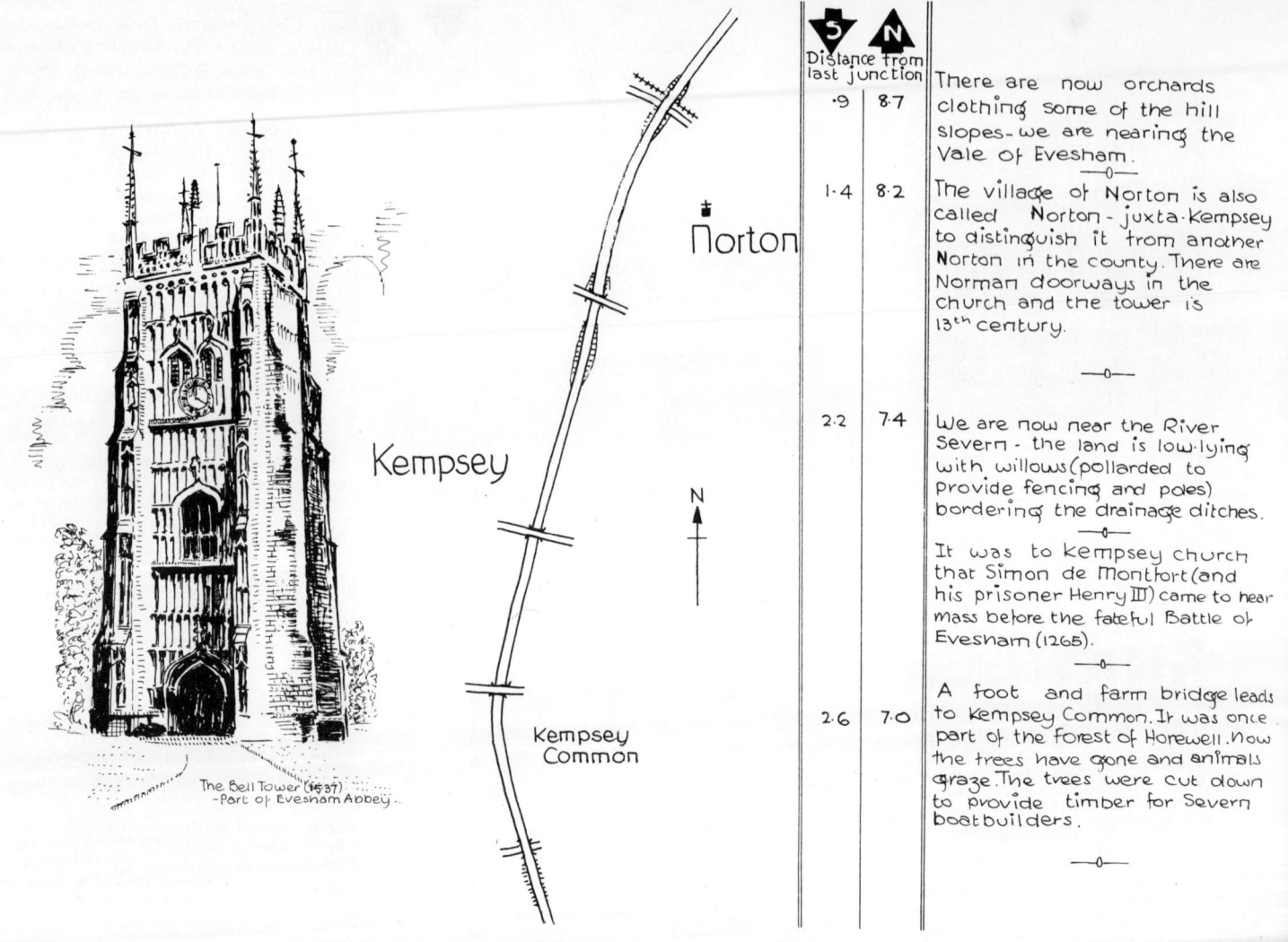

Distance from last junction		
S	N	
.9	8.7	There are now orchards clothing some of the hill slopes – we are nearing the Vale of Evesham.
1.4	8.2	The village of Norton is also called Norton-juxta-Kempsey to distinguish it from another Norton in the county. There are Norman doorways in the church and the tower is 13th century.
2.2	7.4	We are now near the River Severn – the land is low-lying with willows (pollarded to provide fencing and poles) bordering the drainage ditches.
		It was to Kempsey church that Simon de Montfort (and his prisoner Henry III) came to hear mass before the fateful Battle of Evesham (1265).
2.6	7.0	A foot and farm bridge leads to Kempsey Common. It was once part of the forest of Horewell. Now the trees have gone and animals graze. The trees were cut down to provide timber for Severn boatbuilders.

The Bell Tower (1537) – Part of Evesham Abbey

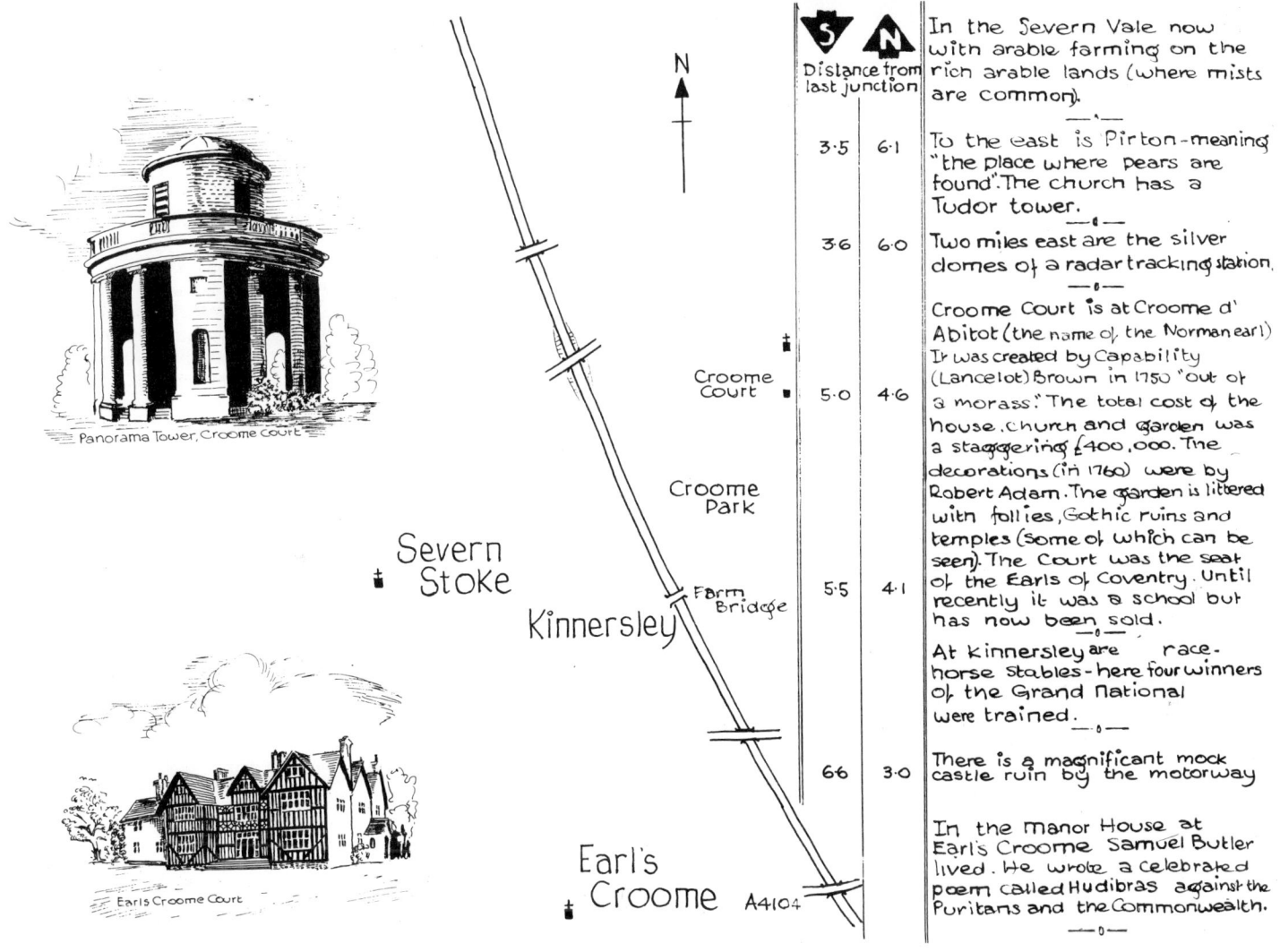

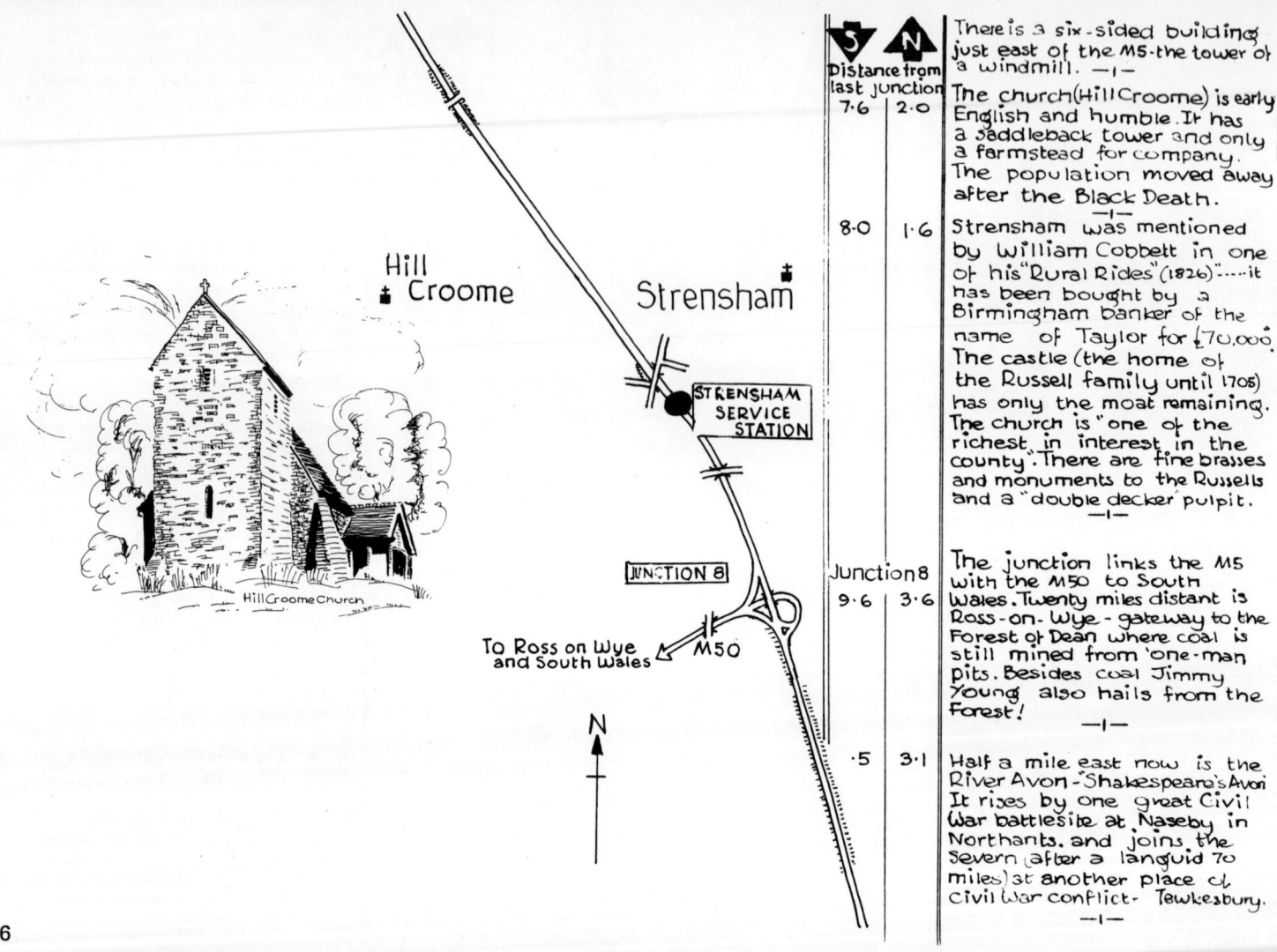

S Distance from last junction	N	
		There is a six-sided building just east of the M5 - the tower of a windmill.
7.6	2.0	The church (Hill Croome) is early English and humble. It has a saddleback tower and only a farmstead for company. The population moved away after the Black Death.
8.0	1.6	Strensham was mentioned by William Cobbett in one of his "Rural Rides" (1826)..... it has been bought by a Birmingham banker of the name of Taylor for £70,000. The castle (the home of the Russell family until 1705) has only the moat remaining. The church is "one of the richest in interest in the county". There are fine brasses and monuments to the Russells and a "double decker" pulpit.
Junction 8 9.6	3.6	The junction links the M5 with the M50 to South Wales. Twenty miles distant is Ross-on-Wye - gateway to the Forest of Dean where coal is still mined from 'one-man pits. Besides coal Jimmy Young also hails from the Forest!
.5	3.1	Half a mile east now is the River Avon - Shakespeare's Avon. It rises by one great Civil War battlesite at Naseby in Northants. and joins the Severn (after a languid 70 miles) at another place of Civil War conflict - Tewkesbury.

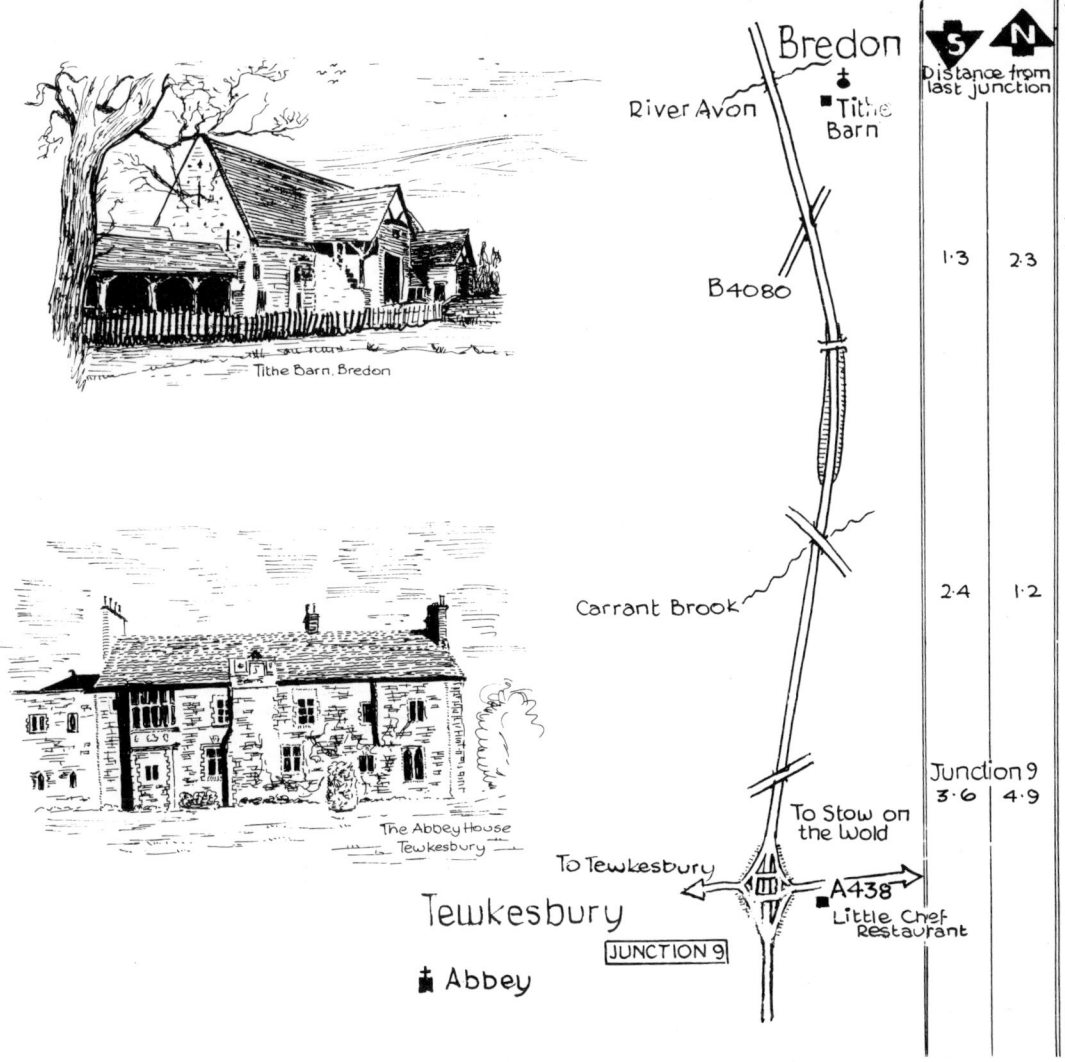

Distance from last junction	
S	N
1.3	2.3
2.4	1.2
Junction 9 3.6	4.9

The eastern horizon is now dominated by Bredon Hill, immortalised by Housman's verse 'In summertime on Bredon'. The hill is a limestone outlier of the Cotswolds and almost tops 1000ft. Mr. Parson in the late 18th century built a folly tower on the summit to make the 1000ft!

—/—

The Tithe Barn in Bredon village has recently been restored after an arson attack. It dates from the 14th century and is owned by the National Trust. The slender spire of St Giles' Church rises to 161ft and was known to John Masefield "...all the land from Ludlow Town to Bredon spire" he wrote.

—/—

Take a final look at Bredon Hill rather than switch on the radio for a weather forecast. The local rhyme runs:-
 "When Bredon Hill puts on his cap,
 Ye men of the Vale beware of that".

Over the Carrant Brook (the county boundary) the motorway enters Gloucestershire.

—/—

Junction 9 - the A438 east leads to the Cotswolds and Stow. To the west is Tewkesbury with its magnificent Abbey. The tower is Norman as are the huge 900 year old pillars in the nave. The Abbey escaped destruction at the Dissolution of the Monasteries. How? By the local folk purchasing it to allow it to escape the clutches of Henry VIII.

—/—

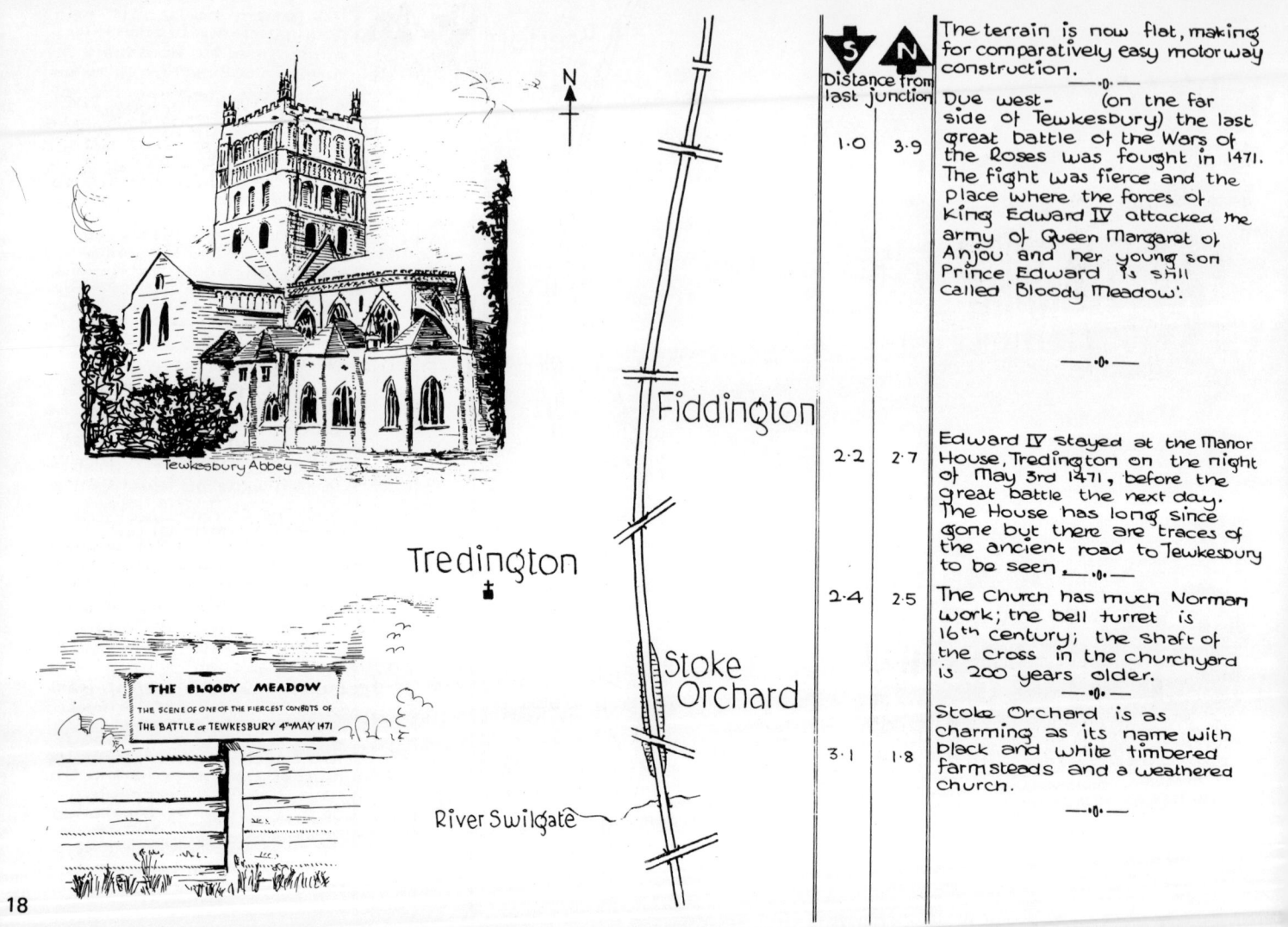

Distance from last junction	
S	N
1.0	3.9
2.2	2.7
2.4	2.5
3.1	1.8

The terrain is now flat, making for comparatively easy motorway construction.

—·0·—

Due west— (on the far side of Tewkesbury) the last great battle of the Wars of the Roses was fought in 1471. The fight was fierce and the place where the forces of King Edward IV attacked the army of Queen Margaret of Anjou and her young son Prince Edward is still called 'Bloody Meadow'.

—·0·—

Edward IV stayed at the Manor House, Tredington on the night of May 3rd 1471, before the great battle the next day. The House has long since gone but there are traces of the ancient road to Tewkesbury to be seen.

—·0·—

The Church has much Norman work; the bell turret is 16th century; the shaft of the cross in the churchyard is 200 years older.

—·0·—

Stoke Orchard is as charming as its name with black and white timbered farmsteads and a weathered church.

—·0·—

The Promenade Cheltenham

Pittville Pump Room Cheltenham

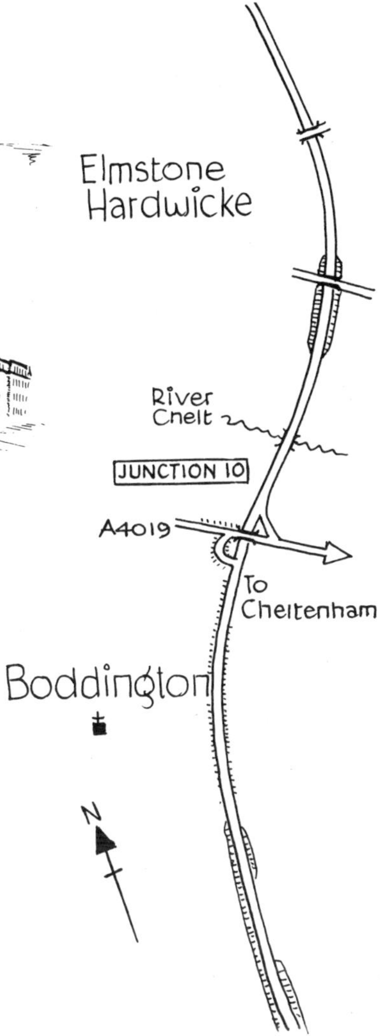

Elmstone Hardwicke

River Chelt

JUNCTION 10

A4019

To Cheltenham

Boddington

Distance from last junction S	N	
4.0	.9	The motorway divides the parish of Elmstone Hardwicke. The tower of the church is old but it is the many leering gargoyles that are so distinctive.
4.6	.3	The stream is the tiny River Chelt.
Junction 10 4.9	3.1	From junction 10 the A4019 goes to the spa town of Cheltenham. There are 16 miles of tree-lined streets to add grace to the town of Regency houses and terraces - to walk along the Promenade is to see one of the most attractive streets in the land. Parks and public gardens cover over 200 acres. The first saline springs were found in 1716. The place was then a large village but by the turn of that century had grown to a large, fashionable town. The accolade of royal patronage came in 1788 when George III came with his family for a holiday.
.5	2.6	Boddington has a manor house that was the target of the Royalists in the Civil War. There is a bell in the church that is over 500 years old.

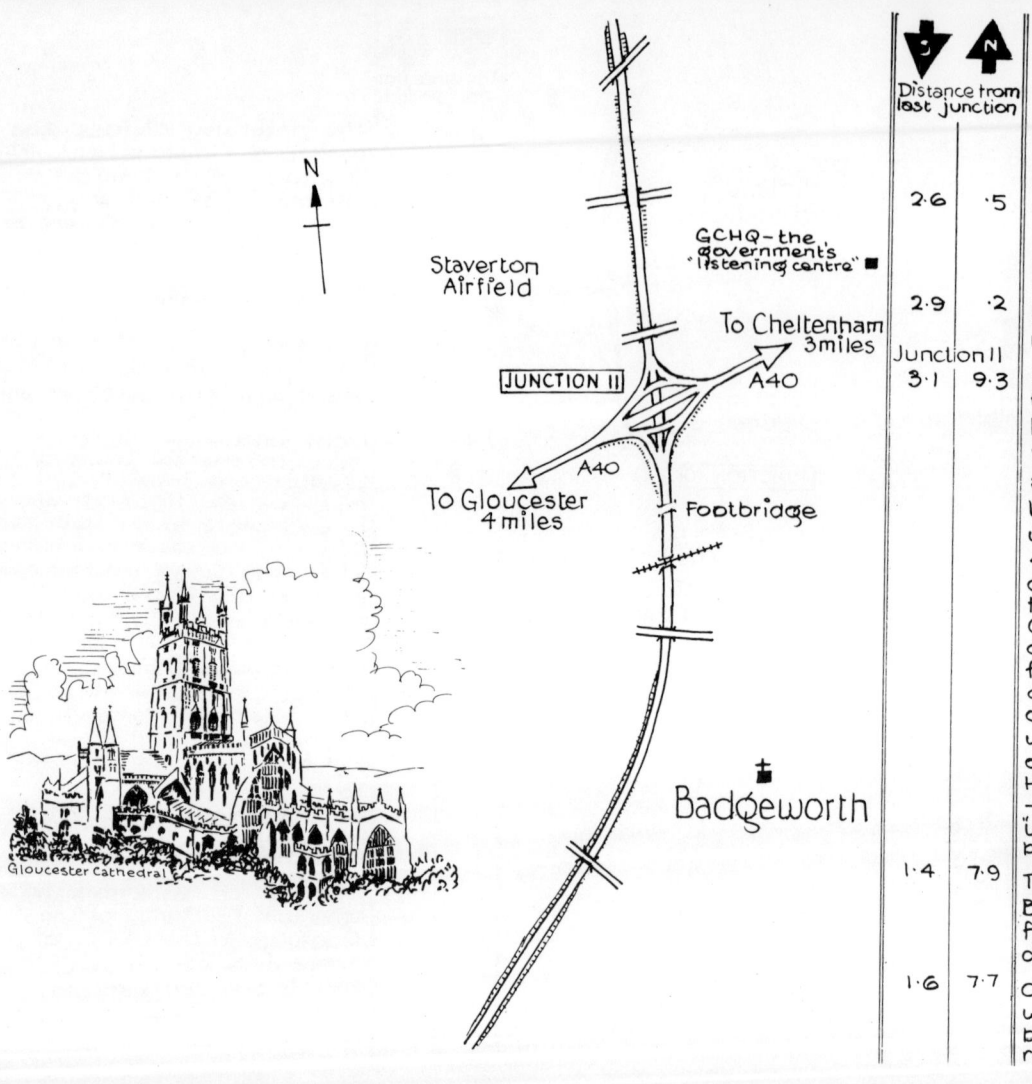

▼S	▲N
Distance from last junction	
2.6	.5
2.9	.2
Junction 11	
3.1	9.3
1.4	7.9
1.6	7.7

Staverton Airfield is near the motorway west – it serves Cheltenham and Gloucester. On the industrial estate aircraft undercarriages are made.

Sleek motorcars end on the scrapheap eventually. The motorway passes a car graveyard.

At junction 11 the A40 goes to Gloucester. Almost alone of English medieval towns it has virtually no traces of the ancient walls. During the Civil War Charles I was at the gates with his Royalist troops and the 4-week siege began. The small garrison of Parliamentarians forced the enemy to retreat. Charles II never forgave the citizens for opposing his father and ordered the destruction of the walls. The crowning glory of the cathedral was started by the Normans on a Saxon site in 1089. However, the old building is encased – in the 15th century the Perpendicular "upright" style of architecture was born here with the lovely fan-vaulting

The church tower we see is at Badgeworth. The building dates from 1315 and is known for its decorative ballflower tracery.

Chosen Hill (500ft) is ½ mile west. Here was a Roman fort. The Normans built a church and nearby is a reservoir for Gloucester.

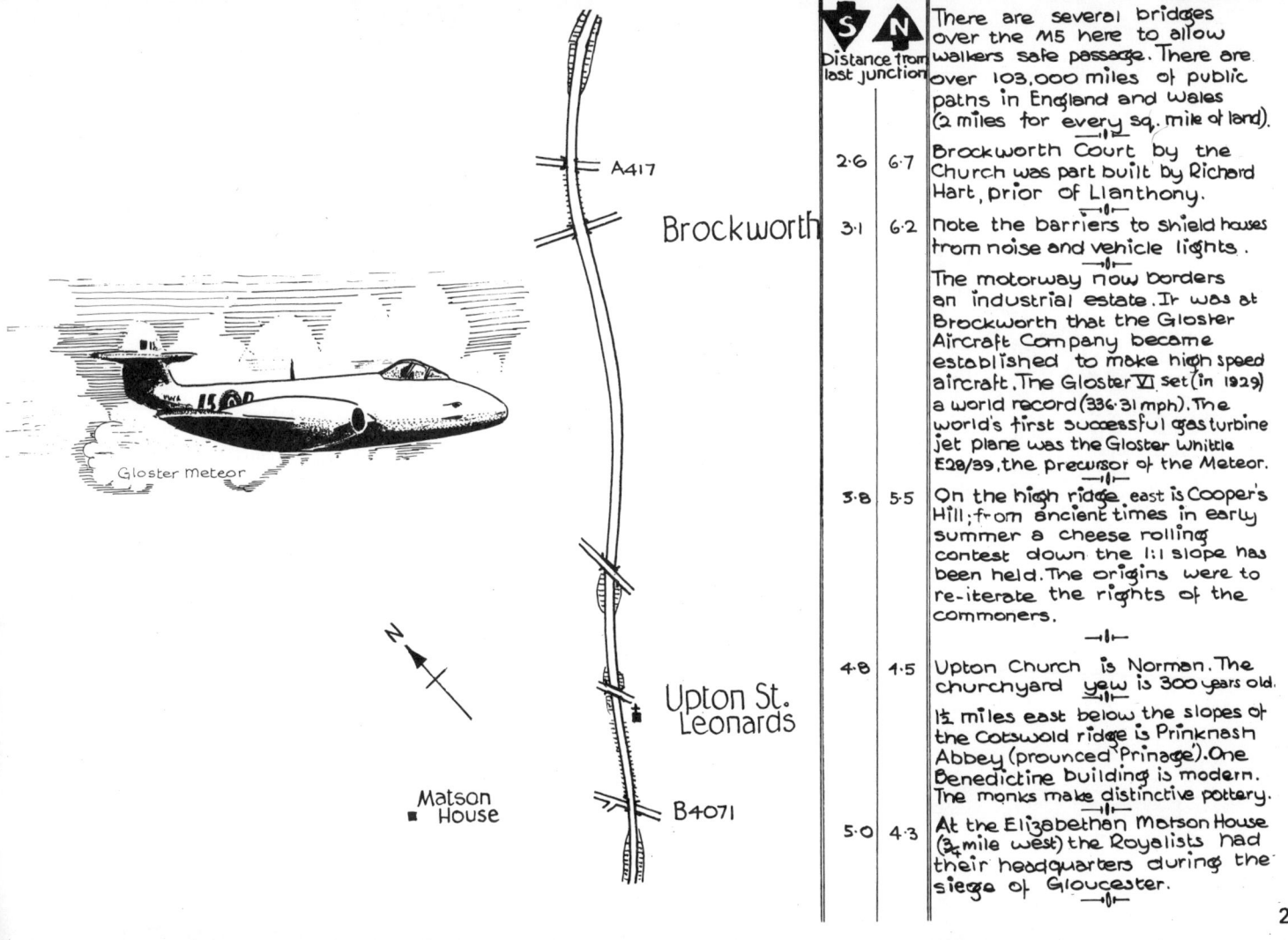

S	N	
Distance from last junction		
		There are several bridges over the M5 here to allow walkers safe passage. There are over 103,000 miles of public paths in England and Wales (2 miles for every sq. mile of land).
2.6	6.7	Brockworth Court by the Church was part built by Richard Hart, prior of Llanthony.
3.1	6.2	Note the barriers to shield houses from noise and vehicle lights.
		The motorway now borders an industrial estate. It was at Brockworth that the Gloster Aircraft Company became established to make high speed aircraft. The Gloster VI set (in 1929) a world record (336.31 mph). The world's first successful gas turbine jet plane was the Gloster Whittle E28/39, the precursor of the Meteor.
3.8	5.5	On the high ridge east is Cooper's Hill; from ancient times in early summer a cheese rolling contest down the 1:1 slope has been held. The origins were to re-iterate the rights of the commoners.
4.8	4.5	Upton Church is Norman. The churchyard yew is 300 years old.
		1½ miles east below the slopes of the Cotswold ridge is Prinknash Abbey (prounced 'Prinage'). One Benedictine building is modern. The monks make distinctive pottery.
5.0	4.3	At the Elizabethan Matson House (¾ mile west) the Royalists had their headquarters during the siege of Gloucester.

21

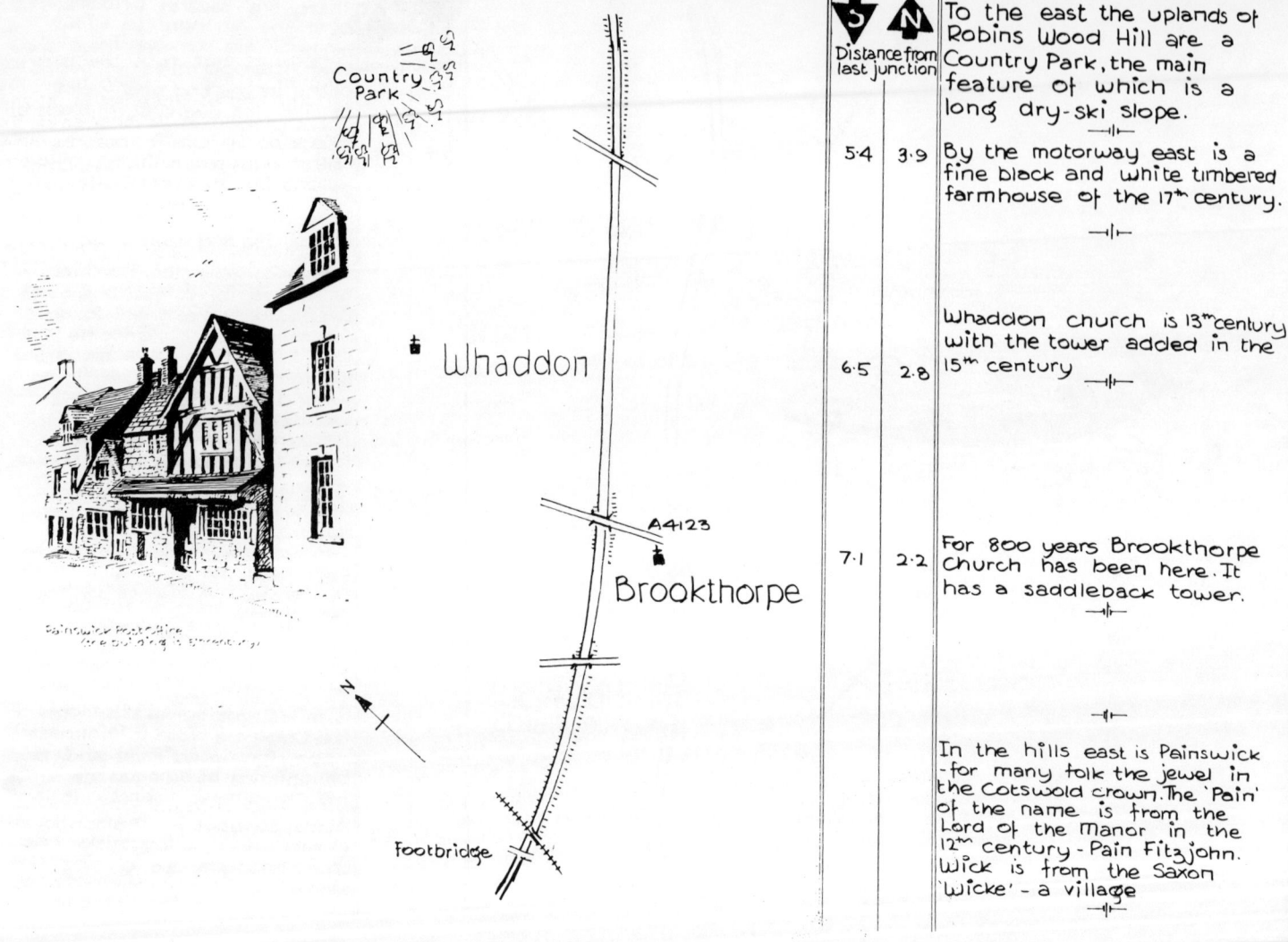

S / N Distance from last junction		
		To the east the uplands of Robins Wood Hill are a Country Park, the main feature of which is a long dry-ski slope.
5.4	3.9	By the motorway east is a fine black and white timbered farmhouse of the 17th century.
6.5	2.8	Whaddon church is 13th century with the tower added in the 15th century
7.1	2.2	For 800 years Brookthorpe Church has been here. It has a saddleback tower.
		In the hills east is Painswick - for many folk the jewel in the Cotswold crown. The 'Pain' of the name is from the Lord of the Manor in the 12th century - Pain Fitzjohn. Wick is from the Saxon 'Wicke' - a village

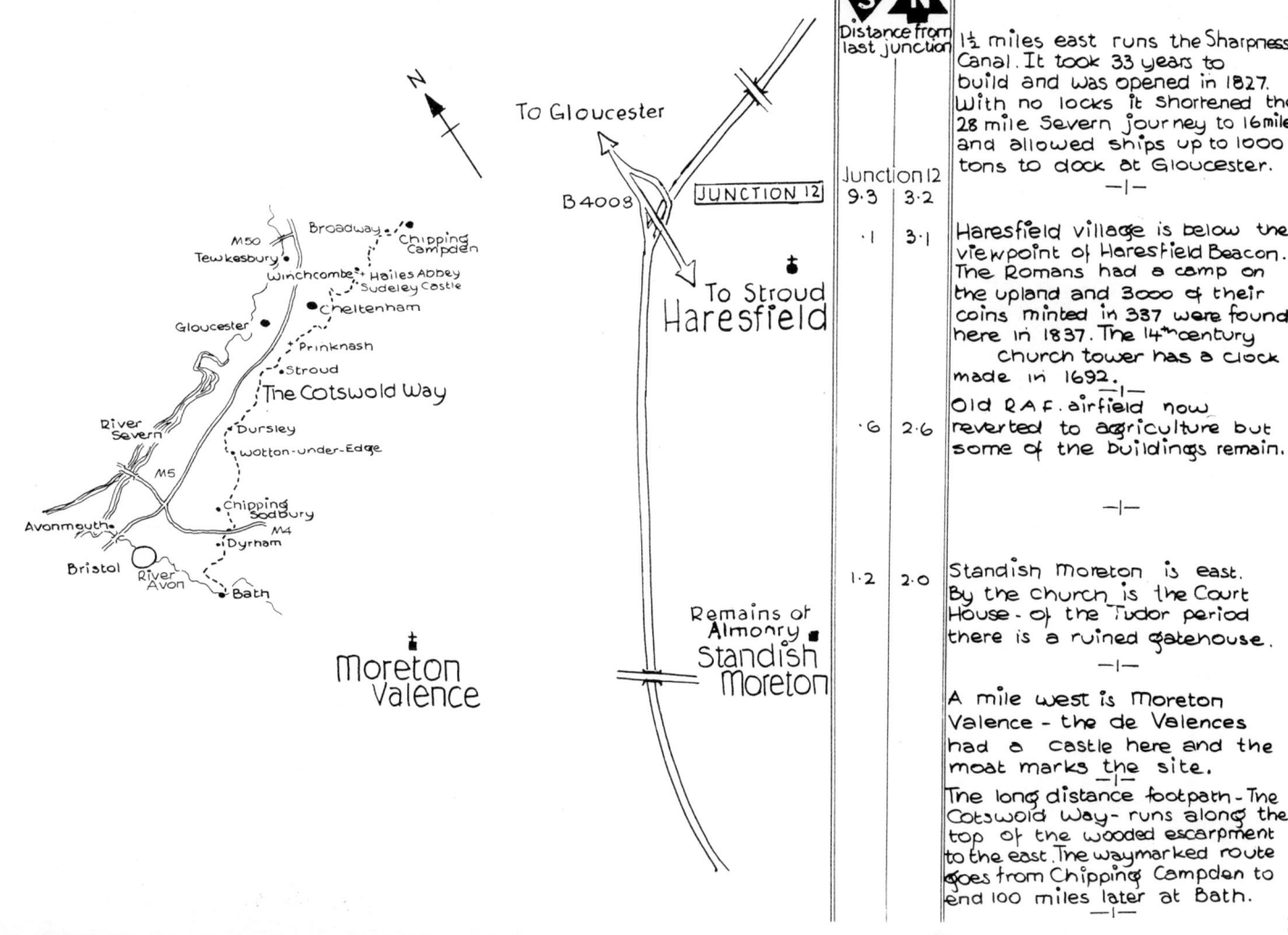

	S	N
	Distance from last junction	
Junction 12	9.3	3.2
	.1	3.1
	.6	2.6
	1.2	2.0

1½ miles east runs the Sharpness Canal. It took 33 years to build and was opened in 1827. With no locks it shortened the 28 mile Severn journey to 16 miles and allowed ships up to 1000 tons to dock at Gloucester.
—1—

Haresfield village is below the viewpoint of Haresfield Beacon. The Romans had a camp on the upland and 3000 of their coins minted in 337 were found here in 1837. The 14th century church tower has a clock made in 1692.
—1—

Old R.A.F. airfield now reverted to agriculture but some of the buildings remain.
—1—

Standish Moreton is east. By the church is the Court House - of the Tudor period there is a ruined gatehouse.
—1—

A mile west is Moreton Valence - the de Valences had a castle here and the moat marks the site.
—1—
The long distance footpath - The Cotswold Way - runs along the top of the wooded escarpment to the east. The waymarked route goes from Chipping Campden to end 100 miles later at Bath.
—1—

23

Whitminster

Whitminster Church

Whooper Swans at the Wildfowl Trust, Slimbridge

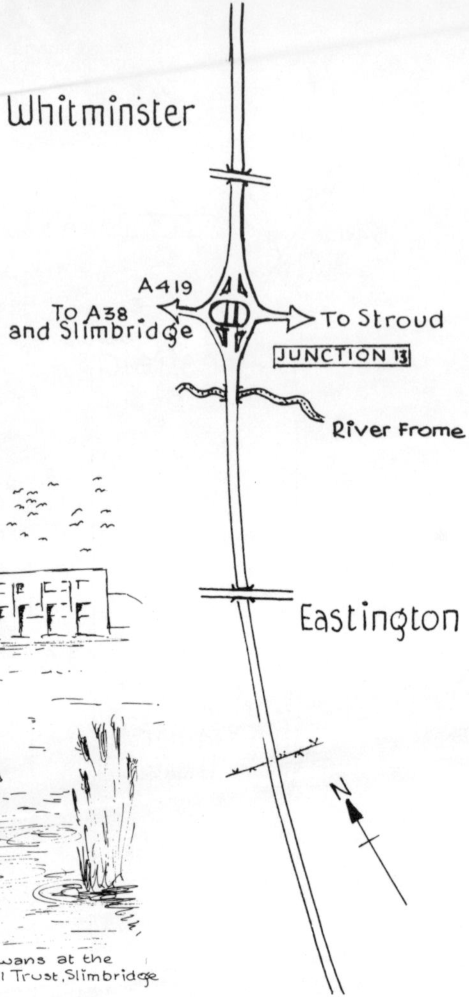

Distance from last junction	
S	N
Junction 13	
3.2	10.6
.3	10.3
1.8	8.5

Two miles above Stroud is the village of Slad, made famous by Laurie Lee when he described his childhood days there in "Cider with Rosie". The 15th tower of Whitminster Church has many weird gargoyles.

From junction 13 the Severn Wildfowl Trust at Slimbridge can be reached via the A38. Here many fascinating hours can be spent observing hundreds of species of birds, many of them rare. There is also a Youth Hostel.

The valley of the River Frome cuts into the Cotswold limestone. The waters helped develop the Gloucestershire cloth trade, they were just right for washing and dyeing wool. It was in the 16th century that the rapid increase in trade came, (due in part to the arrival of skilled Flemish workers). The heyday of the "West of England" cloth was in the 19th century when there were 150 mills on the River Frome, most powered by water.

Two miles east at Leonard Stanley is an interesting group of buildings that includes a tithe barn, the old Saxon church (now part of a farm) and the Norman church that once was incorporated in St. Leonard's Priory.

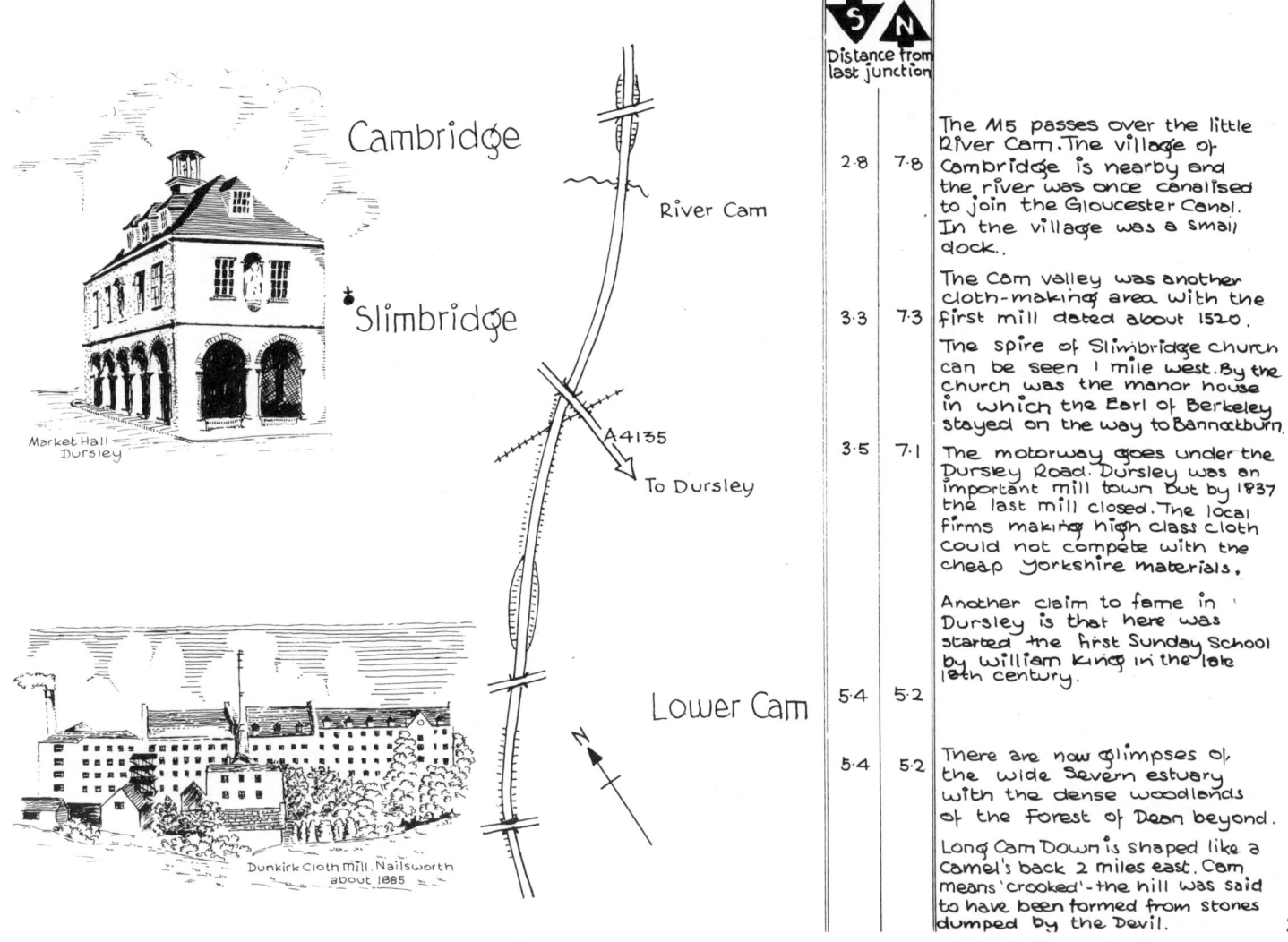

S	N	
\multicolumn{2}{c}{Distance from last junction}	
2.8	7.8	The M5 passes over the little River Cam. The village of Cambridge is nearby and the river was once canalised to join the Gloucester Canal. In the village was a small dock.
3.3	7.3	The Cam valley was another cloth-making area with the first mill dated about 1520.
3.5	7.1	The spire of Slimbridge church can be seen 1 mile west. By the church was the manor house in which the Earl of Berkeley stayed on the way to Bannockburn. The motorway goes under the Dursley Road. Dursley was an important mill town but by 1837 the last mill closed. The local firms making high class cloth could not compete with the cheap Yorkshire materials. Another claim to fame in Dursley is that here was started the first Sunday School by William King in the late 18th century.
5.4	5.2	
5.4	5.2	There are now glimpses of the wide Severn estuary with the dense woodlands of the Forest of Dean beyond. Long Cam Down is shaped like a Camel's back 2 miles east. Cam means 'crooked' - the hill was said to have been formed from stones dumped by the Devil.

Market Hall Dursley

Dunkirk Cloth mill, Nailsworth about 1885

25

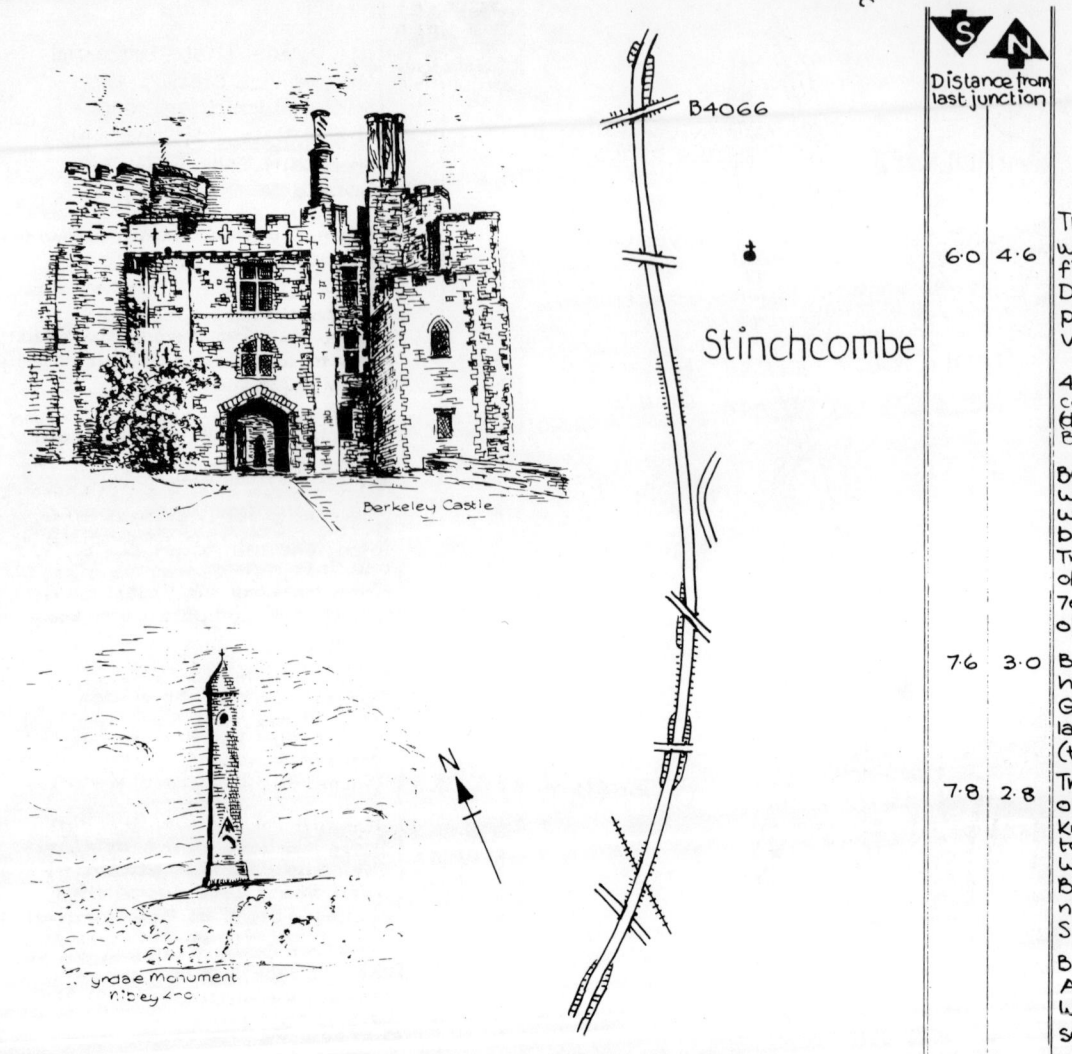

Distance from last junction		
S	N	
6.0	4.6	The village of Stinchcombe with a 14th century church is finely situated below the 700ft Drakestone Point - a promontory plateau where there are wide views through 240°.
		4 miles east is Britain's first commercial nuclear power station (dating from the early 1960's) at Berkeley. Two miles closer is Berkeley Castle where Edward II was murdered in 1327. His body was taken to Gloucester for burial in the Abbey church. The castle has been the home of the Berkeley family for over 700 years. Nearby are the kennels of the Berkeley Hunt.
7.6	3.0	By North Nibley church (on the hills 1 mile eastwards) is Nibley Green - here was fought the last private battle between armies, (the Berkeleys and Warwicks (1471)
7.8	2.8	There is a tall tower in woods on the Cotswolds east at Nibley Knoll. This was erected in 1866 to mark the birthplace of William Tyndale, translator of the Bible. However all in vain - it is now thought he was born at Slimbridge in 1485!
		By Nibley Knoll was an Iron Age camp - and go to nearby Westridge Woods in springtime to see the finest show of bluebells.

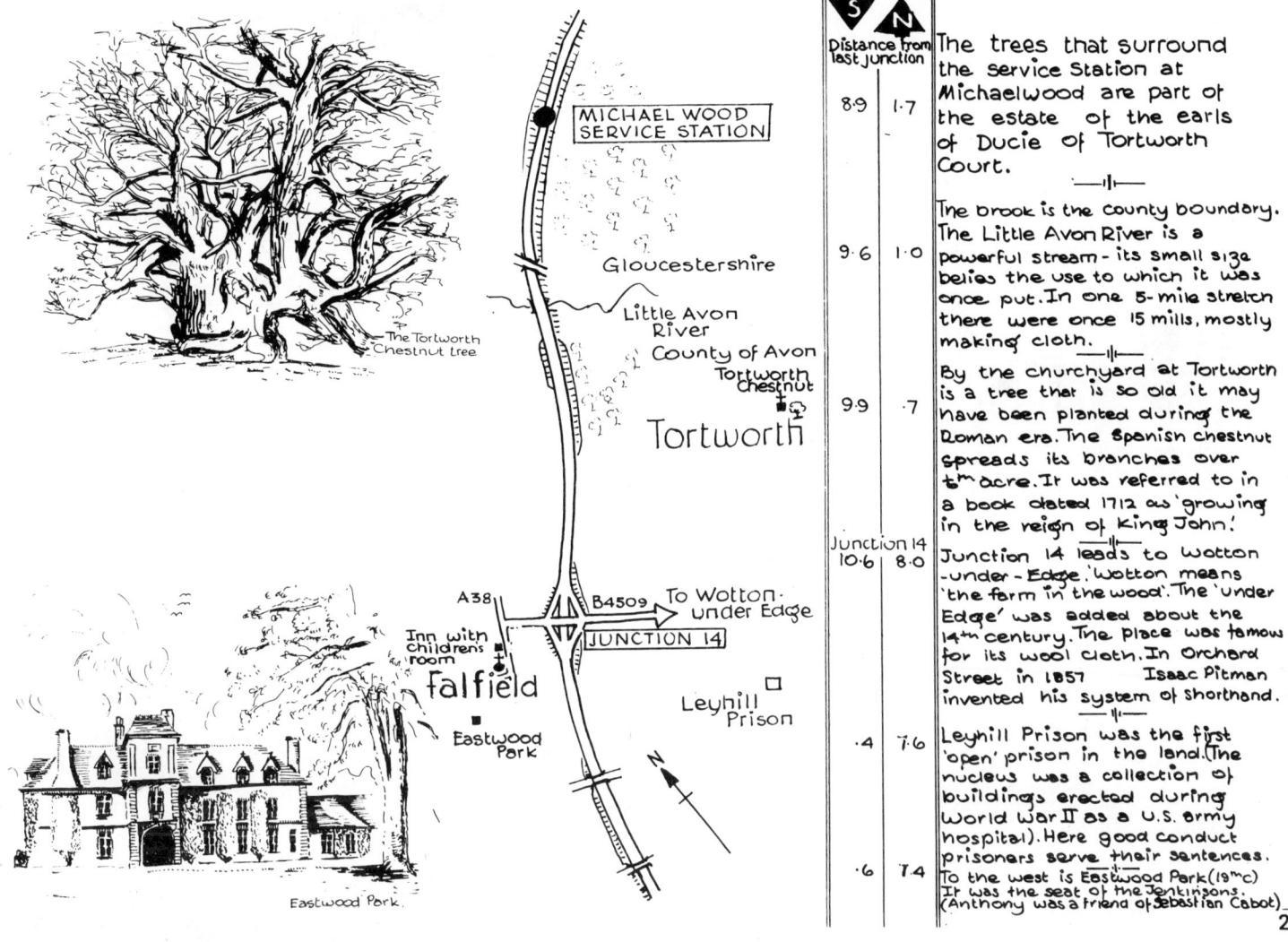

Distance from last junction	
S	N
8.9	1.7
9.6	1.0
9.9	.7
Junction 14 10.6	8.0
.4	7.6
.6	7.4

The trees that surround the service station at Michaelwood are part of the estate of the earls of Ducie of Tortworth Court.

—·||·—

The brook is the county boundary. The Little Avon River is a powerful stream – its small size belies the use to which it was once put. In one 5-mile stretch there were once 15 mills, mostly making cloth.

—·||·—

By the churchyard at Tortworth is a tree that is so old it may have been planted during the Roman era. The Spanish chestnut spreads its branches over ⅙th acre. It was referred to in a book dated 1712 as 'growing in the reign of King John.'

Junction 14 leads to Wotton-under-Edge. 'Wotton means 'the farm in the wood'. The 'under Edge' was added about the 14th century. The place was famous for its wool cloth. In Orchard Street in 1857 Isaac Pitman invented his system of shorthand.

—·||·—

Leyhill Prison was the first 'open' prison in the land. (The nucleus was a collection of buildings erected during World War II as a U.S. army hospital). Here good conduct prisoners serve their sentences.

To the west is Eastwood Park (19thc). It was the seat of the Jenkinsons. (Anthony was a friend of Sebastian Cabot)

27

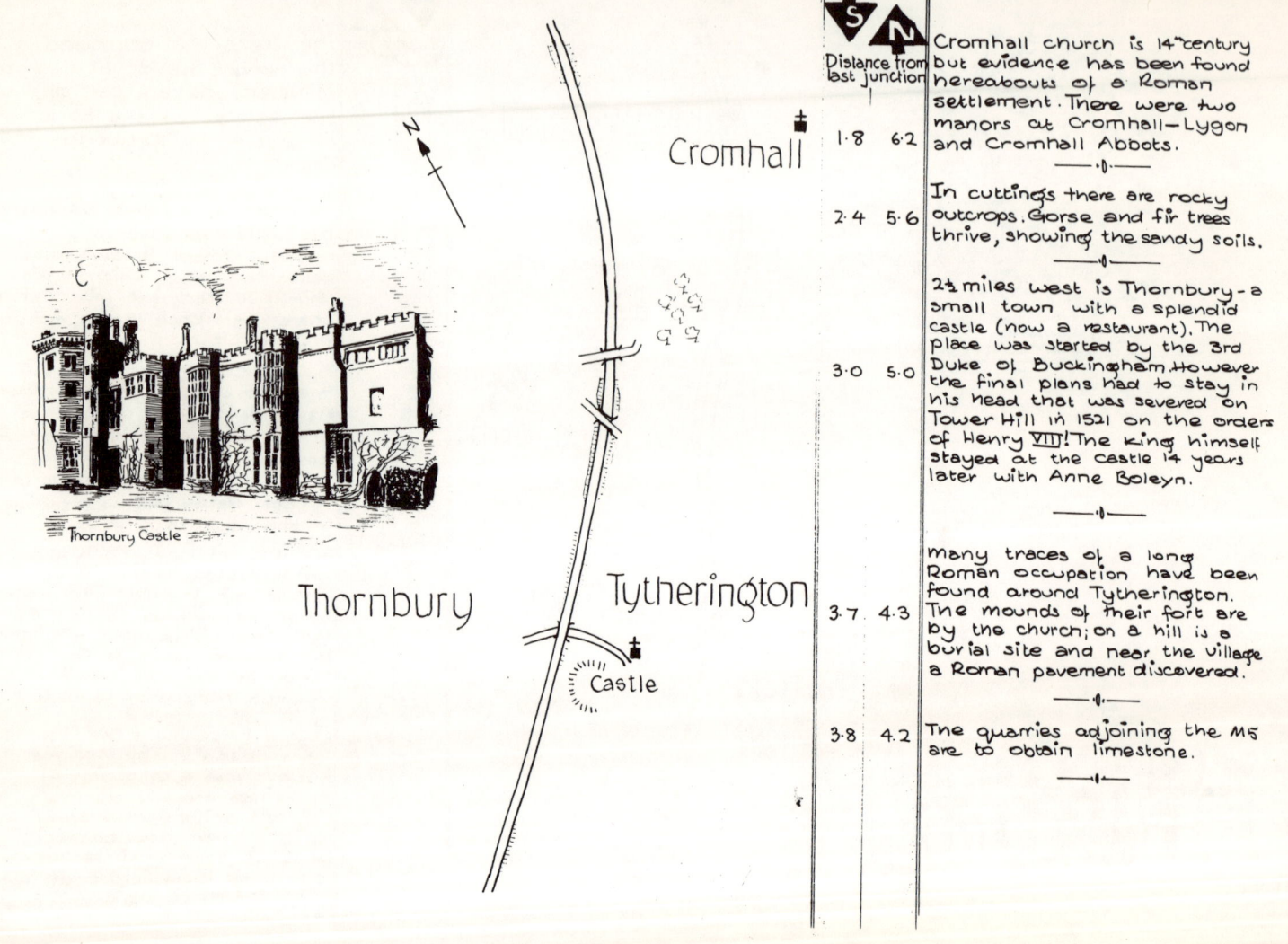

Distance from last junction	
Cromhall	
1.8	6.2

Cromhall church is 14th century but evidence has been found hereabouts of a Roman settlement. There were two manors at Cromhall — Lygon and Cromhall Abbots.

2.4	5.6

In cuttings there are rocky outcrops. Gorse and fir trees thrive, showing the sandy soils.

3.0	5.0

2½ miles west is Thornbury — a small town with a splendid castle (now a restaurant). The place was started by the 3rd Duke of Buckingham. However the final plans had to stay in his head that was severed on Tower Hill in 1521 on the orders of Henry VIII! The King himself stayed at the castle 14 years later with Anne Boleyn.

Thornbury

Tytherington
Castle

3.7	4.3

Many traces of a long Roman occupation have been found around Tytherington. The mounds of their fort are by the church; on a hill is a burial site and near the village a Roman pavement discovered.

3.8	4.2

The quarries adjoining the M5 are to obtain limestone.

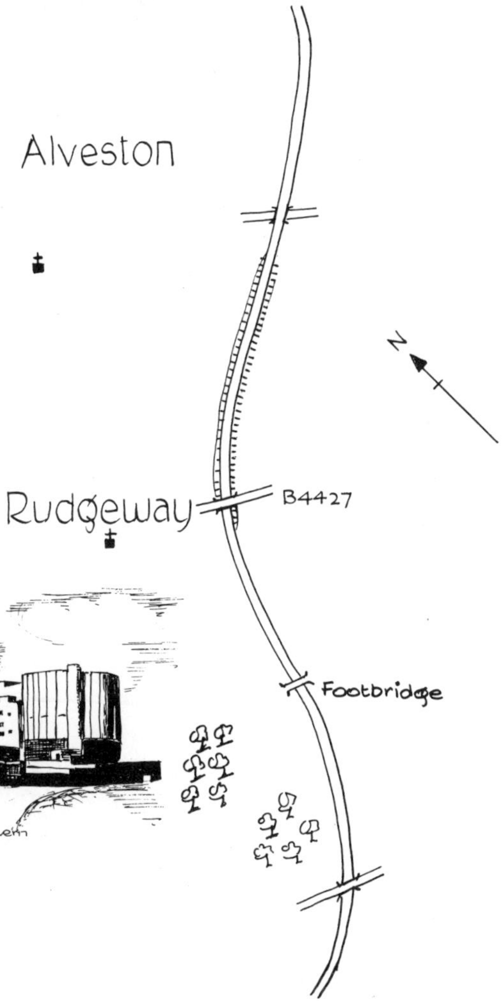

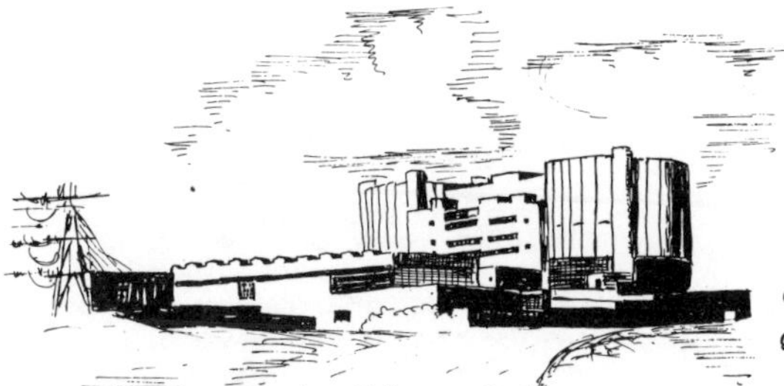

S	N	
Distance from last junction		
4.9	3.1	Alveston (Alwin's stone) and not to be confused with Olveston or Alf's place just south) is a dormitory town. There was rapid expansion at the turn of the century and a new church was built in 1885. North-West is Oldbury Nuclear Power Station that has supplied electricity to the National Grid since 1949.
5.4	2.6	The old church for Alveston keeps a 17th century farm company at Rudgeway. The medieval building is now only a shell.
6.4	1.6	Small coppices for wildlife are to the west. Eastwards is a large pastoral plain where dairy farming predominates. A feature of the area is the pattern of seven electricity power lines radiating from one distribution point.

Nuclear Power Station – Oldbury-on-Severn

29

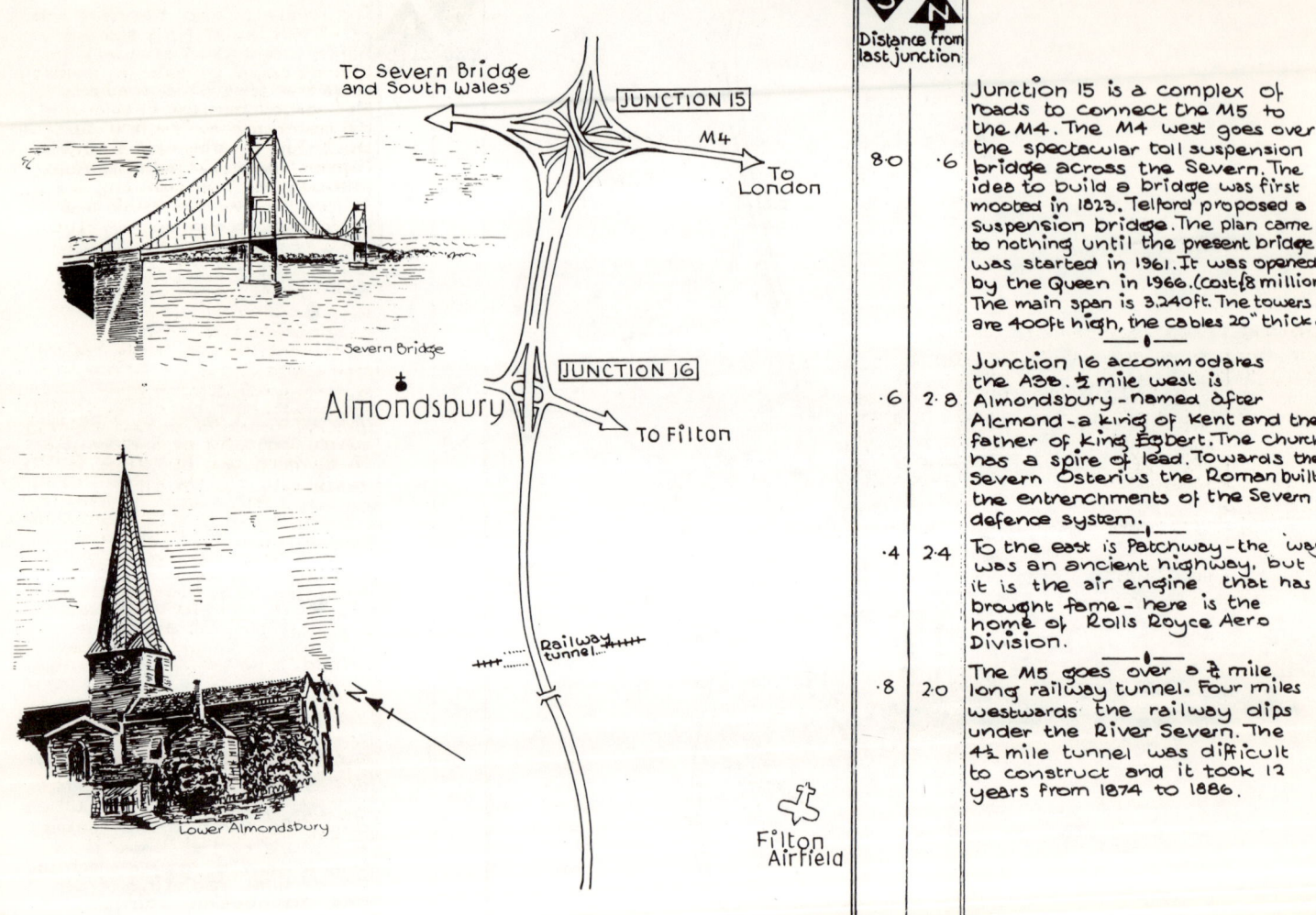

Distance from last junction		
8.0	.6	Junction 15 is a complex of roads to connect the M5 to the M4. The M4 west goes over the spectacular toll suspension bridge across the Severn. The idea to build a bridge was first mooted in 1823. Telford proposed a suspension bridge. The plan came to nothing until the present bridge was started in 1961. It was opened by the Queen in 1966. (Cost £8 million) The main span is 3,240ft. The towers are 400ft high, the cables 20" thick.
.6	2.8	Junction 16 accommodates the A38. ½ mile west is Almondsbury - named after Alcmond - a king of Kent and the father of King Egbert. The church has a spire of lead. Towards the Severn Osterius the Roman built the entrenchments of the Severn defence system.
.4	2.4	To the east is Patchway - the 'way' was an ancient highway, but it is the air engine that has brought fame - here is the home of Rolls Royce Aero Division.
.8	2.0	The M5 goes over a ⅞ mile long railway tunnel. Four miles westwards the railway dips under the River Severn. The 4½ mile tunnel was difficult to construct and it took 12 years from 1874 to 1886.

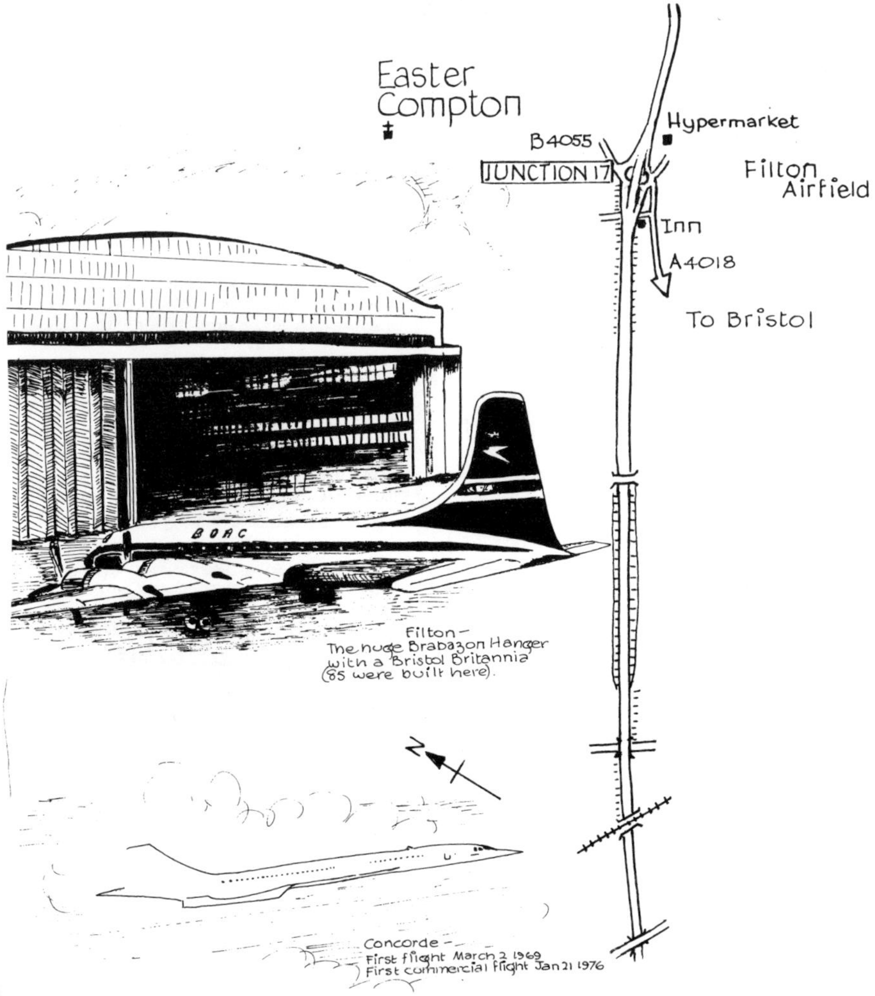

Distance from last junction S	N
2.6	.2
Junction 17	
2.8	3.6

The runways and hangars are at Filton. The airfield started before World War I so work on aircraft could proceed in a nearby large transport depot where Sir George White was chairman of the tram company. The first 'plane was the Bristol Boxkite. 4500 Bristol Fighters (World War I) and Blenheims followed. The Brabazon was a huge failure but the Britannia and Concorde both came from Filton (now part of British Aerospace).

—·ıı·—

Junction 17 is a way to Bristol (once one of the greatest ports in the land. In 1497 the Cabots set out to discover the American continent. The port trade has largely gone elsewhere but Bristol remains a large administrative and manufacturing centre. Its products include tobacco, confectionery, wines, oils and chemicals. There are remains of a Dominican friary in the city but the magnificent church is St Mary Redcliffe, built with the funds of rich merchants (especially William Canynges). The spire is 285 ft high. The cathedral was begun by the Normans as a monastery of St. Augustine; the nave is as recent as the 19° century. A popular city attraction is Brunel's iron ship - the SS Great Britain. It was built in 1843 and returned finally to its home port in 1970; it was restored after serving as a beached coal bunkering vessel in the Falkland Islands for many years. The old theatre in Bristol is the Theatre Royal, considered to be the oldest playhouse still in use in the country; it was built in 1764.

—·ıı·—

Filton —
The huge Brabazon Hanger with a Bristol Britannia (85 were built here).

Concorde —
First flight March 2 1969
First commercial flight Jan 21 1976

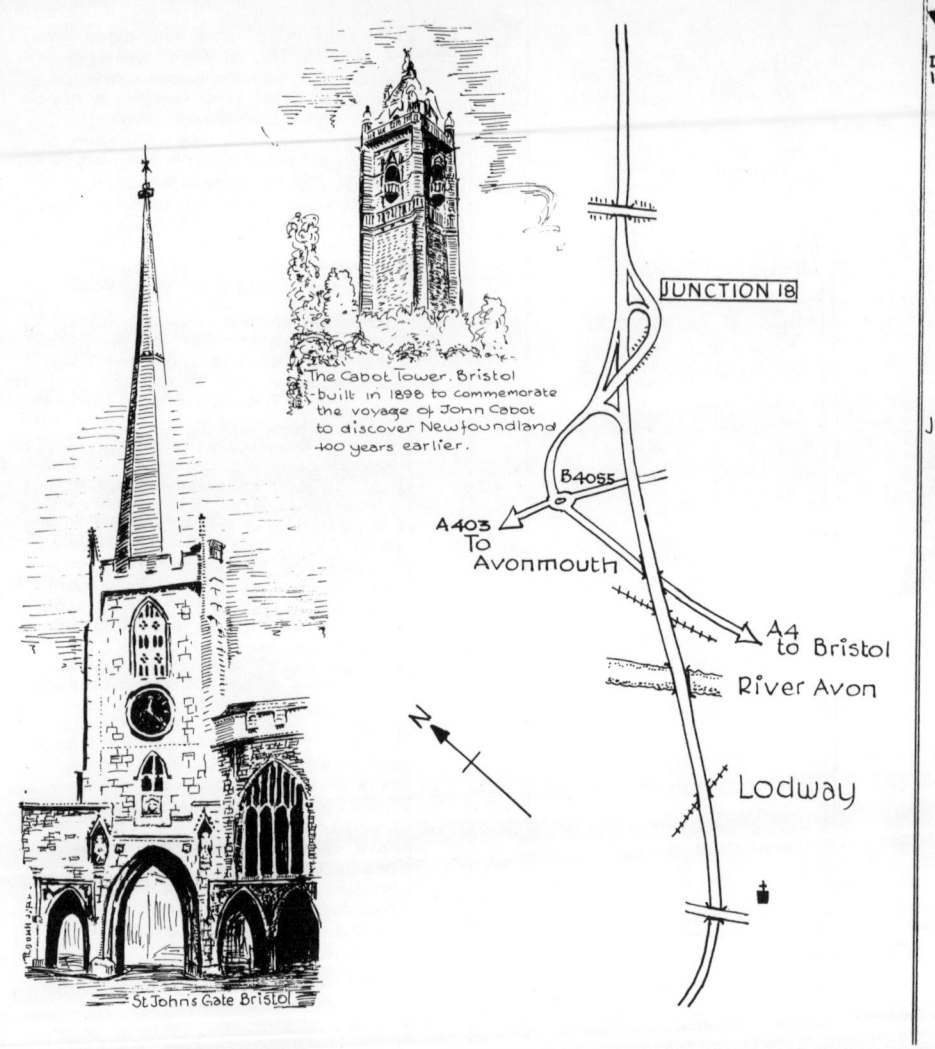

Distance from last junction		
S	N	
3.2	.4	To the west along the banks of the Severn Estuary many huge industries have been established including chemicals (ICI), oils (Shell & BP), grain ("the largest animal-food compounding mill in the world") and metals (zinc). There is a good infrastructure with docks, motorways, railways and a centre of population nearby. —o0o—
Junction 18 3.6	2.3	Besides the important road to Bristol, junction 18 also leads to Avonmouth. The first dock that siphoned trade from Bristol was opened in 1877. The docks in Bristol have a history going back to Saxon days. The slave trade (at first against the law) was important in the 18th century. It was finally declared illegal in 1808. —o0o—
.8	1.5	The "humped-back" bridge over the River Avon was finally opened after many delays in 1974. Its box-girder method of construction was suspect after the collapse of a similar structure in Australia. —o0o—
1.2	1.1	There are glimpses of the Clifton Suspension Bridge (245ft above the Avon 3 miles east). Designed by Brunel, building began in 1831. The funds were exhausted by 1840. In 1859 Brunel died. Another start was not made until 1861. The completed structure cost £100,000. —o0o—

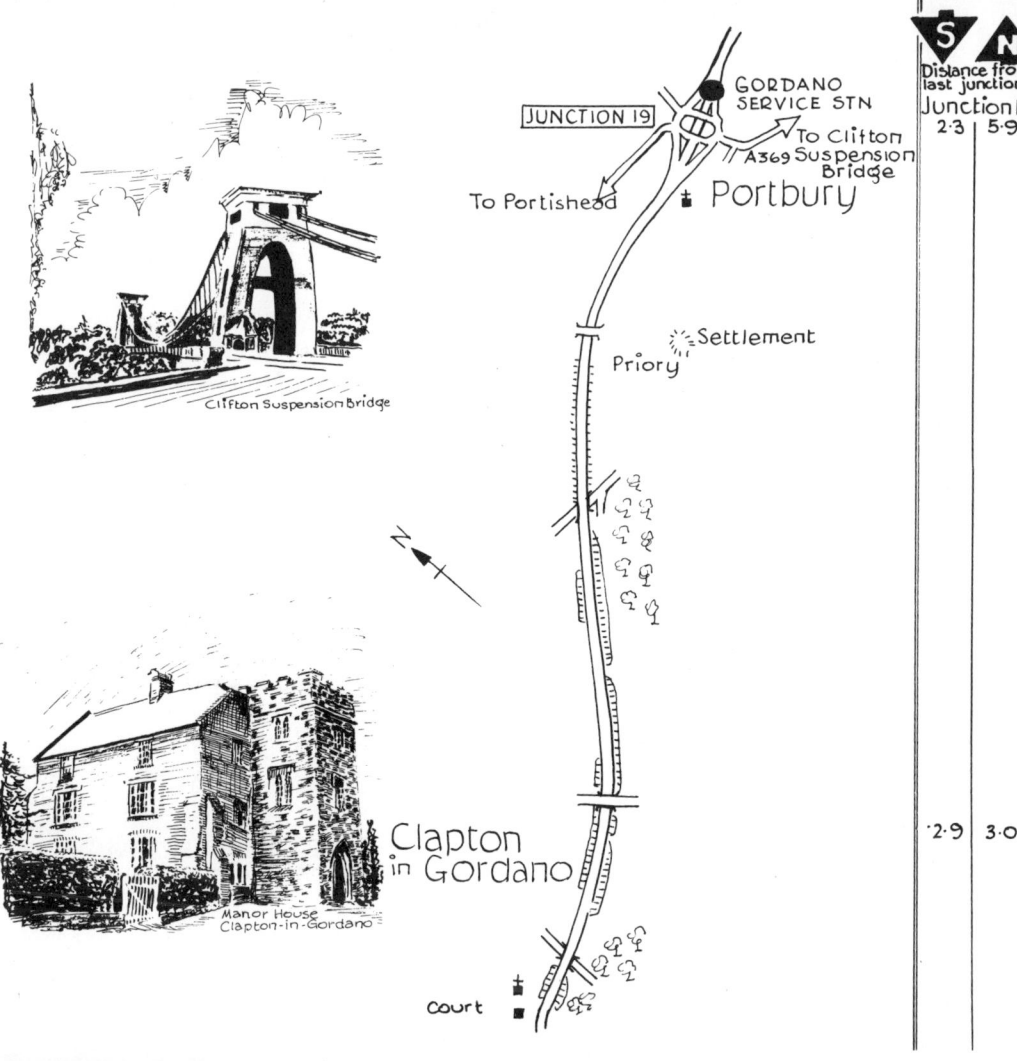

	S	N
Distance from last junction		
Junction 19		
	2.3	5.9
	2.9	3.0

The Gordano Service Station at Junction 19 takes its name from the Gordano Valley. ('Gore' = wedge). The area is squeezed between the limestone ridge by the estuary and the sandstone finger of the Failand ridge. The middle of the valley (once marshland) is covered with a 15ft layer of peat.
—I—

The road west leads to Portishead. The dock here was completed in 1879 after twice collapsing. Portbury Dock (Opened in 1977 by the Queen) has the largest dock gates in Britain.

Portbury Priory was a cell of an Augustinian Abbey – the remains are now incorporated in a residence. The church has some gravestones said to be amongst the oldest in the country (early 17th century).
—I—

The road is now chiselled deep into the side of the edge of the wooded hills giving spectacular views over the Gordano Valley.
—I—

Clapton means 'hill-place'. The village nestles below the scarp edge of the ridge. The manor (Clapton Court) by the Norman church is from the 15th century. This was once an industrial village with coal and iron workings.
—I—

33

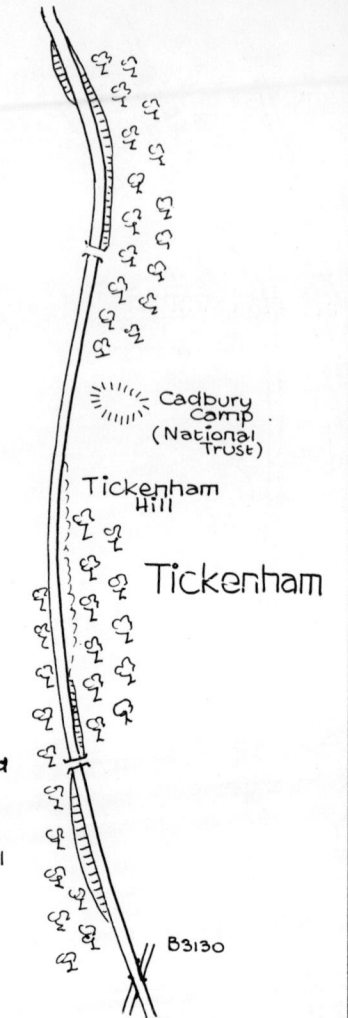

Distance from last junction	
S	N
3.9	2.0
5.5	.4

The motorway still overlooks the valley from some height above the moors ('mor' = Old English for 'open waste ground'). The moors of the Gordano Vale were drained in 1810. The drainage ditches are called 'rhines'.

—|—

Alongside the motorway are the National Trust lands that contain the mounds and trenches of the Iron Age fort Cadbury Camp.

—|—

The village of Tickenham is over the hill south of the M5. It has a church with the unusual dedication to St Quiricus and St. Juliette. There are only two similar churches in the country.

—|—

Court Hill to the north hides Clevedon Court; the old manor house is another National Trust property and was built about 1320. The Elton family lived here from 1709 (when it was purchased by Abraham Elton, a wealthy Bristol merchant) until 1973.

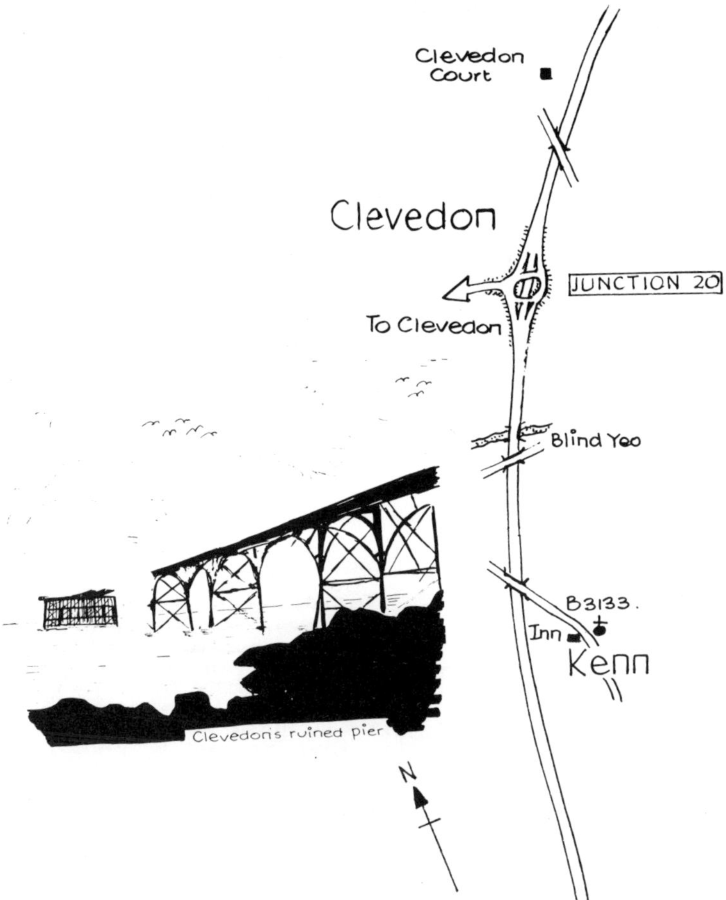

Distance from last junction

S	N
Junction 20	
5.9	5.8
.4	5.4

Just west of the motorway is Clevedon Court — the old manor house of Clevedon that was started in 1320. It was the home of Bristol merchants, the Eltons, until taken over by the National Trust in 1973. Many writers visited the Court including Thackeray and Tennyson.

Junction 20 is the turning for Clevedon. Once mainly a seaside town for retirement it is now (thanks to the motorway) a commuter town for Bristol workers. The town grew rapidly in Victorian times (only 300 people lived here in 1800). The former splendid pier is now forlorn but there are hopes of restoration. It dates from 1869; it was built with rails which Brunel had intended for use on the South Wales Railway.

The M5 goes over the Blind Yeo (a waterway straightened for drainage purposes and to prevent flooding across this low-lying moorland area). Drainage and enclosure (up to the 19th century) transformed the heavy clay moors to good pasture farmland.

The M5 is crossed by the B4133 at Kenn. In a field behind the inn (the Drum and Monkey) the last public hanging in Somerset took place in 1832. The crime was setting fire to corn stacks.

Clevedon's ruined pier

Kingston Seymour

Market Cross Congresbury

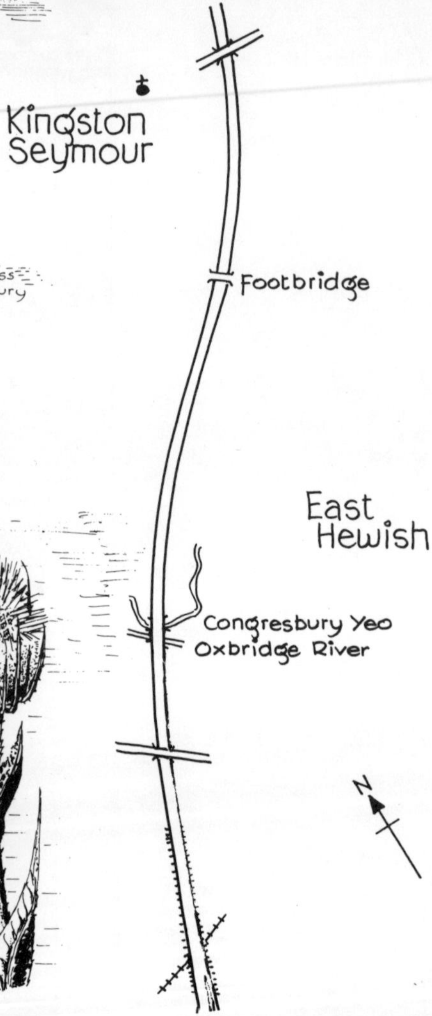

Footbridge

East Hewish

Yatton Church (2 miles east) has a truncated spire.

The Teasel – used to raise the nap on cloth

Congresbury Yeo Oxbridge River

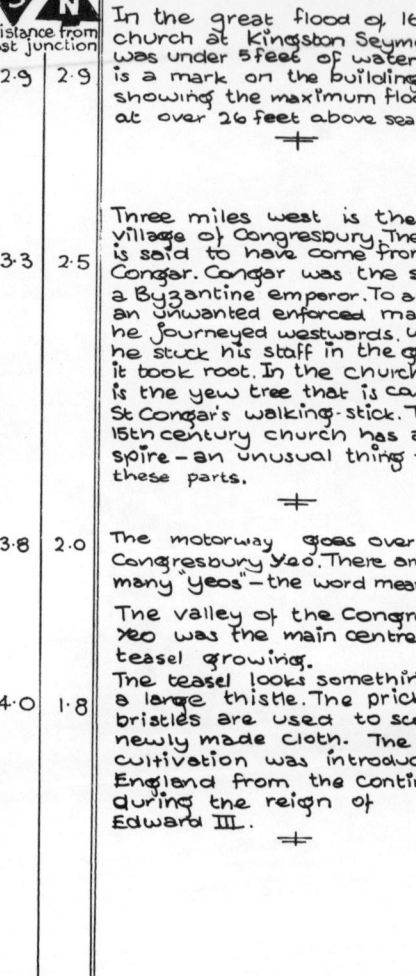

S Distance from last junction	N
2.9	2.9
3.3	2.5
3.8	2.0
4.0	1.8

In the great flood of 1607 the church at Kingston Seymour was under 5 feet of water. There is a mark on the building showing the maximum flood at over 26 feet above sea level.

Three miles west is the village of Congresbury. The name is said to have come from St. Congar. Congar was the son of a Byzantine emperor. To avoid an unwanted enforced marriage he journeyed westwards. When he stuck his staff in the ground it took root. In the churchyard is the yew tree that is called St Congar's walking-stick. The 15th century church has a spire – an unusual thing for these parts.

The motorway goes over the Congresbury Yeo. There are many "Yeos" – the word means 'river'.

The valley of the Congresbury Yeo was the main centre for teasel growing. The teasel looks something like a large thistle. The prickly bristles are used to scour newly made cloth. The cultivation was introduced to England from the continent during the reign of Edward III.

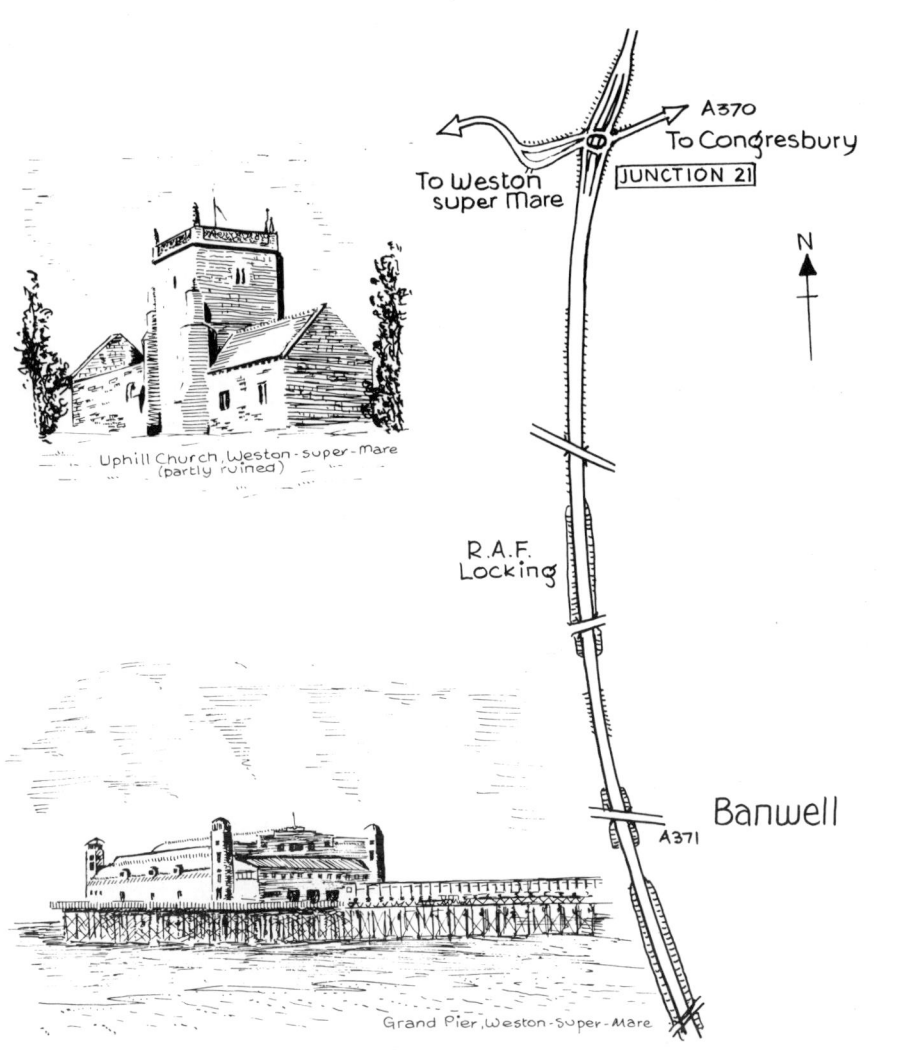

Distance from last junction S	N	
Junction 21		Weston-Super-Mare has little history beyond 200 years. Before that the fishing village had about 100 inhabitants. It was developed by Bristol investors early in the 19th century. The great expansion came with the railway bringing Bristol folk to the seaside. It is now popular with Midlanders who shoot down the M5 at the first glint of sunshine.
5.8	10.0	
.6	9.4	On Worlebury Hill overlooking Weston a windmill tower called 'The Observatory' is perched. The hill was used in the Iron Age as a fort. South of Weston is Brean Down (N.T.). It is known as the main site in Britain for the white rock rose.
1.5	8.5	The R.A.F. station was built on a moor. The village of Locking has a church founded by the monks of Woodspring Priory (near the coast above Weston).
2.0	8.0	Three miles west is the village of Churchill – said to have been the home (Churchill Court) of ancestors of Sir Winston Churchill. By the motorway west are old Ordnance factories where Rolls Royce aero-engines are made.
3.0	7.0	The road is cut through rocky hills – foothills of the limestone Mendips. There was also lead oxide mining in this area. On the hill above Banwell is a cave where an enormous quantity of pre-historic bones (including cave bear, cave lion mammoth and woolly rhinos) were found.

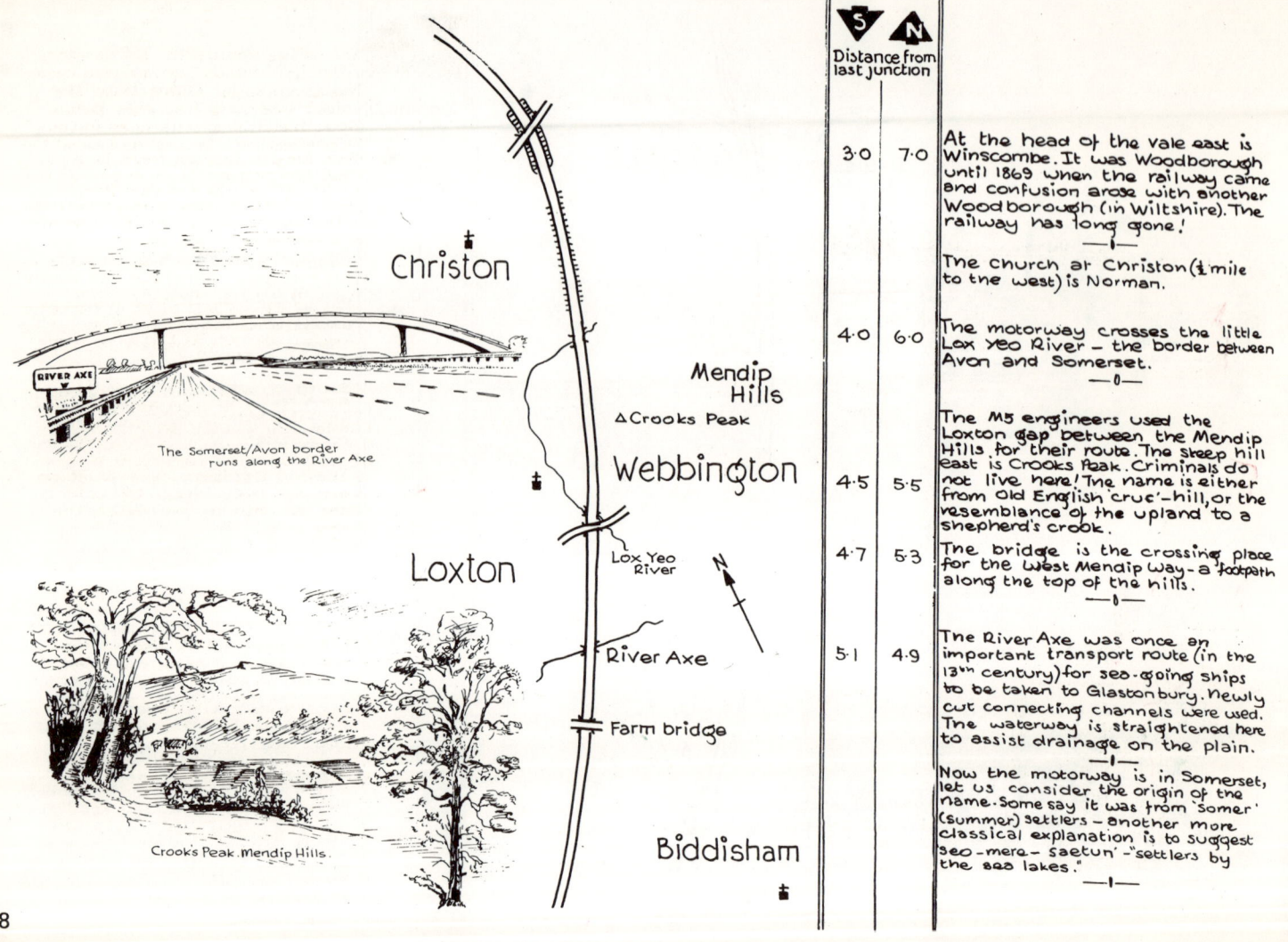

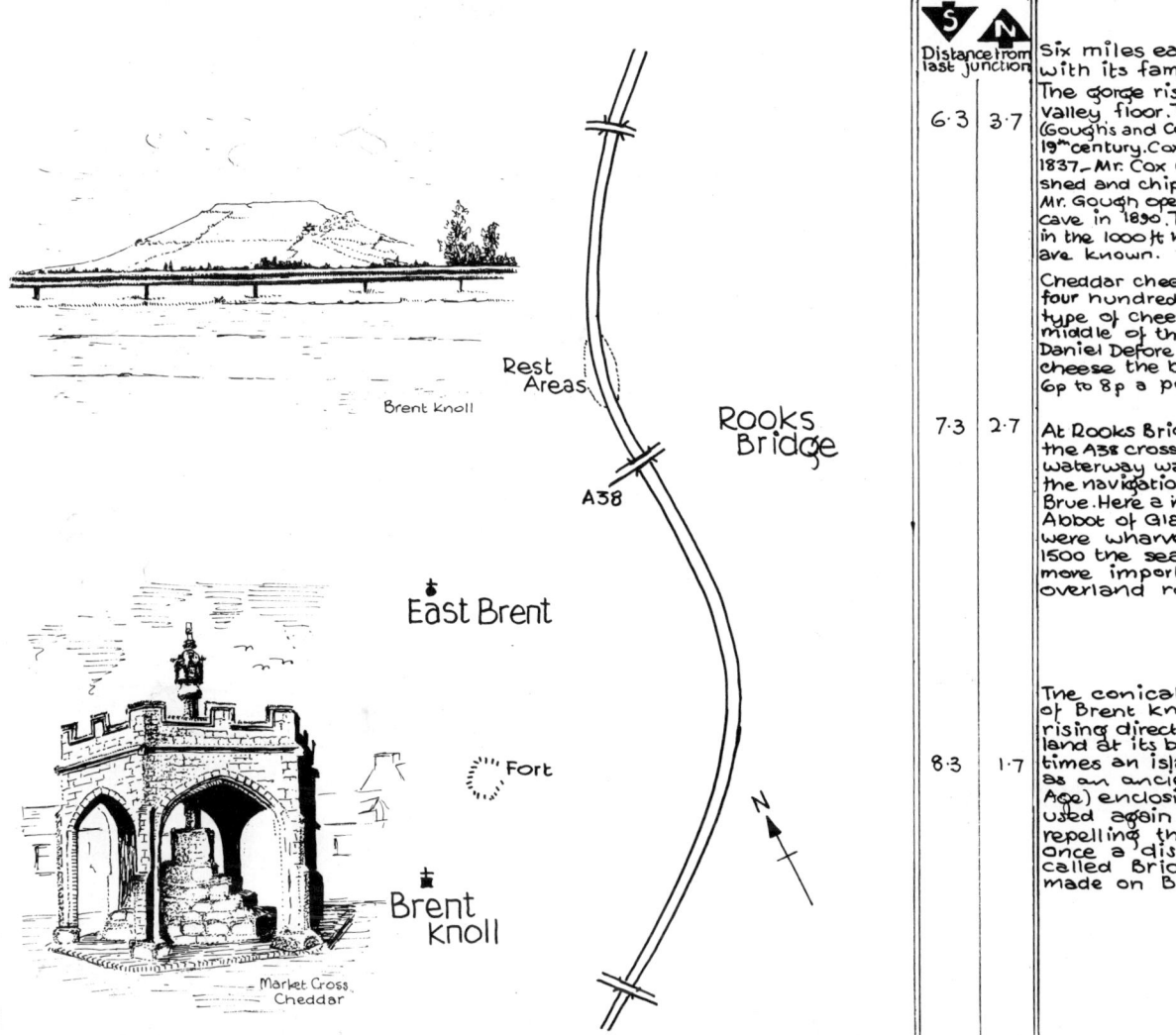

S Distance from last junction	N
6.3	3.7
7.3	2.7
8.3	1.7

Six miles eastwards is Cheddar, with its famous gorge and caves. The gorge rises 480ft. above the valley floor. The two main caves (Gough's and Cox's) were found in the 19th century. Cox's cave came to light in 1837 — Mr. Cox wanted room for a new shed and chipped away at the rockface. Mr. Gough opened and exploited his cave in 1890. There are many other caves in the 1000ft high Mendips — over 400 are known.

—1—

Cheddar cheese has been famous for four hundred years, but the standard type of cheese dates from the middle of the last century. About 1700 Daniel Defoe thought Cheddar cheese the best in England at 6p to 8p a pound!

—1—

At Rooks Bridge — a quiet spot today — the A38 crosses the Mark Yeo. This waterway was constructed to join the navigation of the Rivers Axe and Brue. Here a mill was built by the Abbot of Glastonbury and there were wharves and warehouses. In 1500 the sea route to Bristol was more important than the overland route.

—1—

The conical-shaped landmark of Brent Knoll is 450ft high rising directly from the flat land at its base. It was in ancient times an island and was used as an ancient hill fort (Iron Age) enclosing 4 acres. It was used again by the Saxons repelling the Danish invaders. Once a distinctive cheese called Bridgwater Cheese was made on Brent Knoll's farms.

—1—

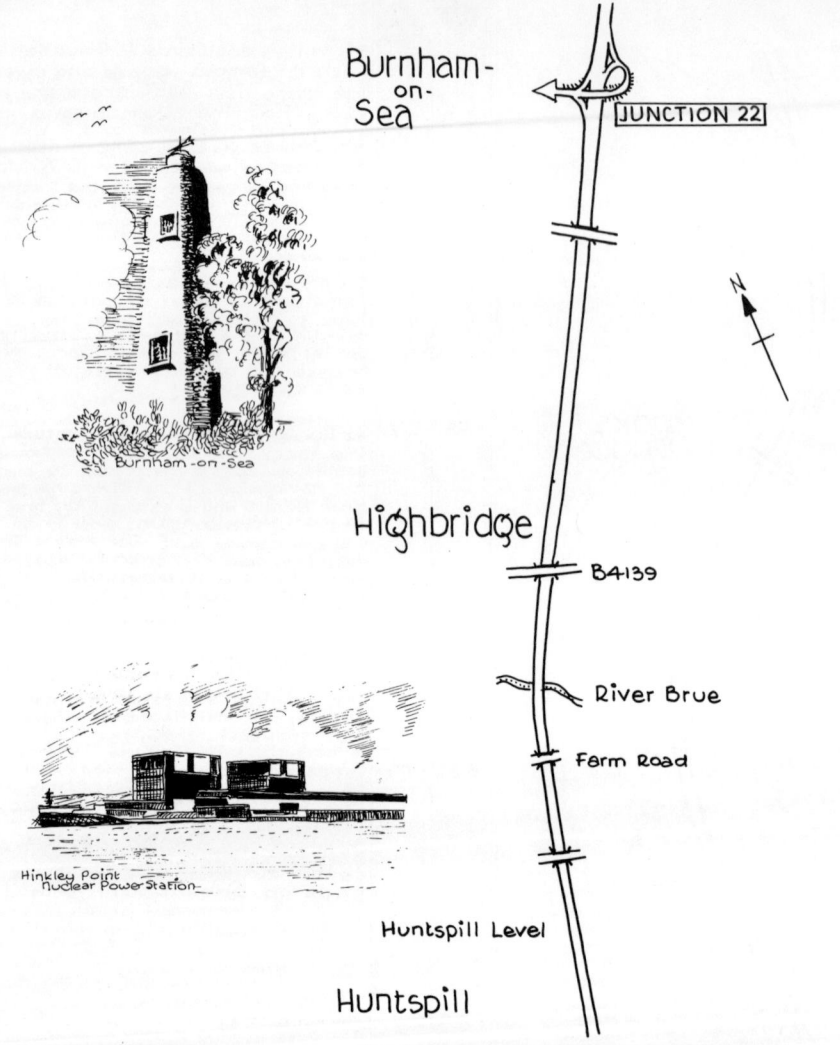

S	N	
Distance from last junction		
10.0	51	Burnham-on-Sea is approached from Junction 22. The place could well be accused under the Trades Description Act! Unless one is fortunate to visit at the time of the two high tides the sea disappears over 2 miles across the mud. Until the late 18th century Burnham was a poverty-stricken village. A curate, the Rev. David Davies, established a small spa using deep well water and the town grew during Victorian times.
Junction 22		
1.3	3.8	We pass a large dairy – the flatlands make good grazing but old industries (teazes for clothmaking and withies for basketmaking) survive.
		The bridge at Highbridge was originally both a bridge and a dam with sluice gates to shut against the incoming tide; thereby large boats could come into the town. Trade further increased by a canal to Glastonbury (1833). The canal did not survive more than 20 years – killed off by the new railways and silt.
1.7	3.4	The first lighthouse at the mouth of the River Brue was built by Burnham's Rev. Davies. The tolls extracted from passing ships provided him with the funds for his spa.
1.9	3.2	We are now deep in the area known as the Somerset Levels. The vast area of peat created stability problems for the motorway builders. The subsidence was minimised by using lightweight coal ash from Aberthaw Power Station. Special railway sidings to transport it to the site were used.

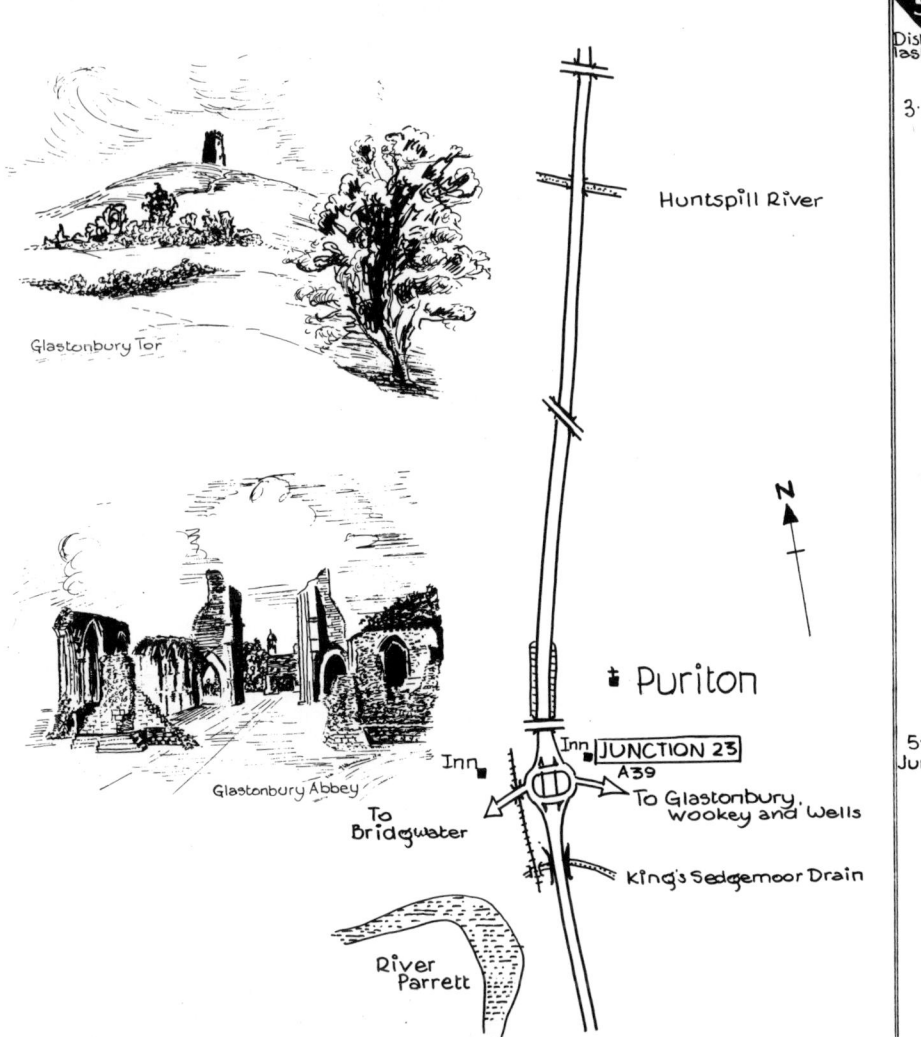

S Distance from last junction	N	
3.3	1.8	The Huntspill River is, in effect, an elongated man-made reservoir, (5 miles in length). It was created in the early 1940's, ostensibly to supply water for a new explosive being produced at Puriton – but also to ease the risk of flooding of the moors (severe floods in 1917, 1919 and 1929).
		5 miles west are the massive coastal towers of the Hinkley Point Nuclear Power Stn. (built 1950).
		Eastward are the vast moors of peat (which is extracted by mechanical diggers). The area is drained by an intricate network of rivers, ditches and drains stretching to the Isle of Avalon on which Glastonbury was built and around which tales of King Arthur are woven.
		A mile west is Pawlett; on the nearby river meadows of Pawlett Hams are some of the finest grazing lands in the county.
		There were salt mines (locally known as the Treacle Mines) until the 1920's; the salt level was at a depth of 650ft.
5.1 Junction 23	4.9	The A39 at junction 23 goes to Glastonbury. On the Tor (500ft above sea level) is a ruined chapel. The town is inextricably linked to the legends of King Arthur. There are the magnificent Abbey ruins – the building was 594ft long. The Glastonbury Thorn, that is said to bloom on Christmas Day, is the subject of a legend – that it is holy and grew from the staff of Joseph of Arimathea when it was stuck in the ground. (The body of Jesus was placed in the garden tomb of Joseph after the Crucifixion).

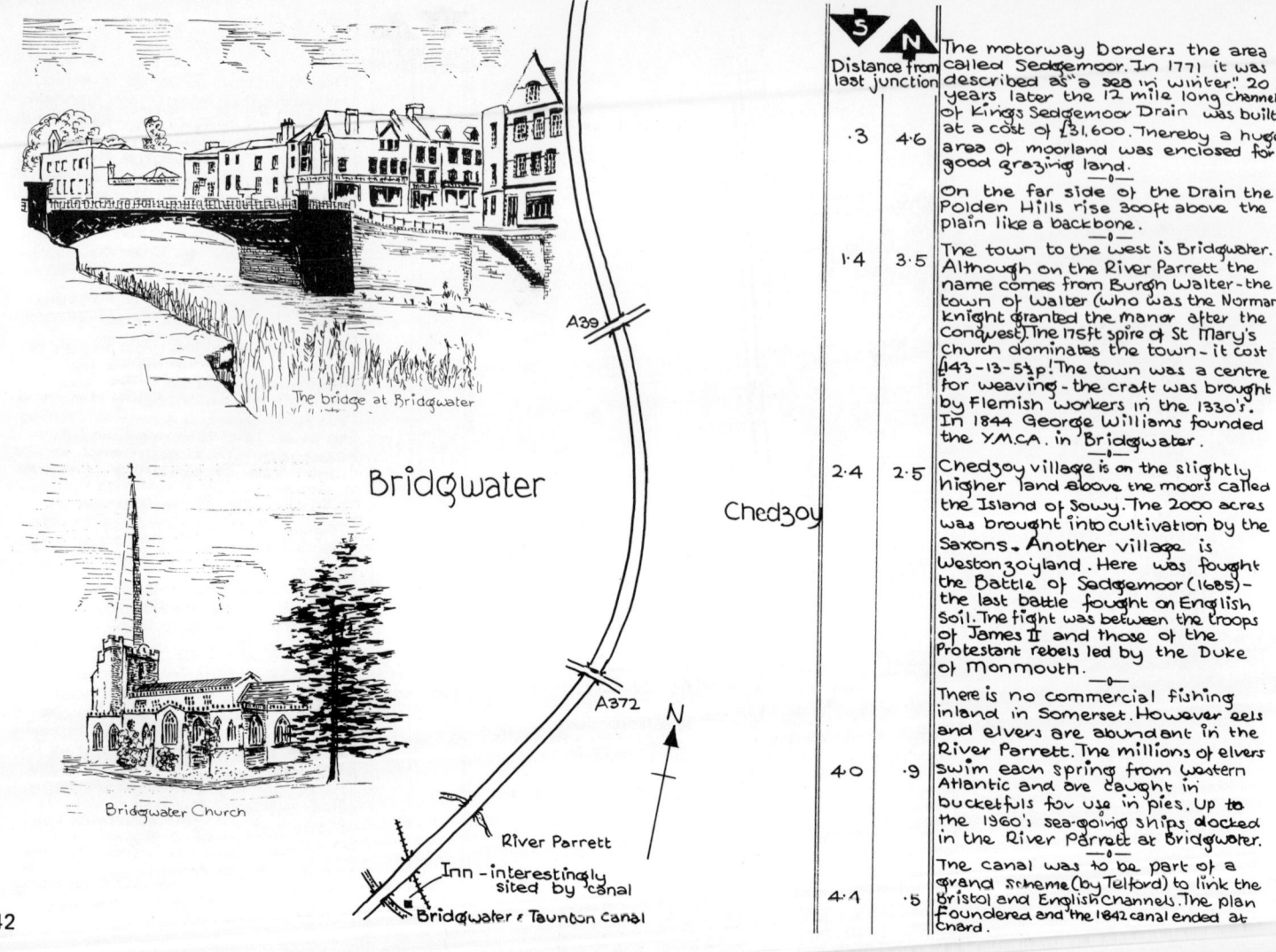

Distance from last junction		
.3	4.6	The motorway borders the area called Sedgemoor. In 1771 it was described as "a sea in winter". 20 years later the 12 mile long channel of Kings Sedgemoor Drain was built at a cost of £31,600. Thereby a huge area of moorland was enclosed for good grazing land.
		On the far side of the Drain the Polden Hills rise 300ft above the plain like a backbone.
1.4	3.5	The town to the west is Bridgwater. Although on the River Parrett the name comes from Burgh Walter – the town of Walter (who was the Norman knight granted the manor after the Conquest). The 175ft spire of St Mary's Church dominates the town – it cost £43-13-5½p! The town was a centre for weaving – the craft was brought by Flemish workers in the 1330's. In 1844 George Williams founded the Y.M.C.A. in Bridgwater.
2.4	2.5	Chedzoy village is on the slightly higher land above the moors called the Island of Sowy. The 2000 acres was brought into cultivation by the Saxons. Another village is Westonzoyland. Here was fought the Battle of Sedgemoor (1685) – the last battle fought on English soil. The fight was between the troops of James II and those of the Protestant rebels led by the Duke of Monmouth.
4.0	.9	There is no commercial fishing inland in Somerset. However eels and elvers are abundant in the River Parrett. The millions of elvers swim each spring from Western Atlantic and are caught in bucketfuls for use in pies. Up to the 1960's sea-going ships docked in the River Parrett at Bridgwater.
4.1	.5	The canal was to be part of a grand scheme (by Telford) to link the Bristol and English Channels. The plan foundered and the 1842 canal ended at Chard.

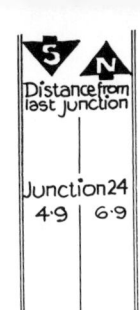

North Petherton Church tower

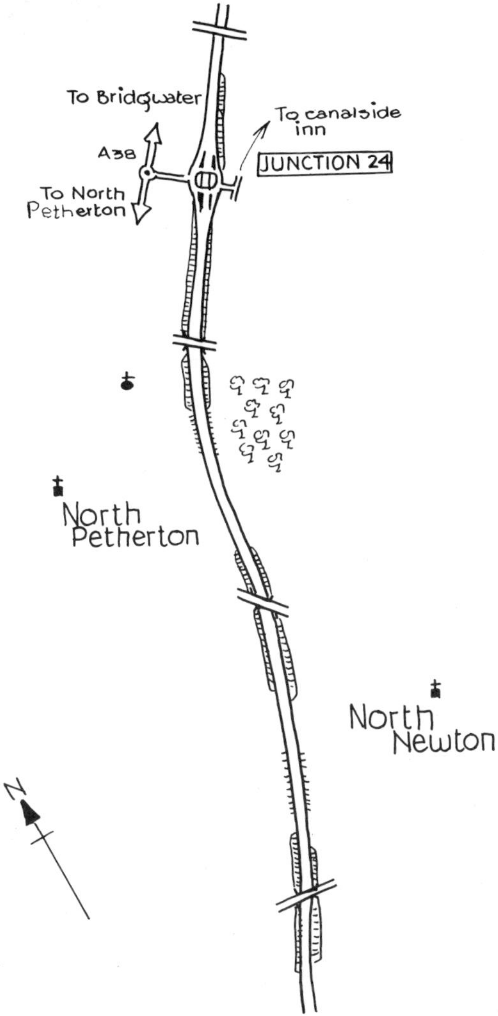

S Distance from last junction	N
Junction 24	
4.9	6.9
.8	6.1
1.0	5.9
1.8	5.1

Junction 24 is another exit to the old Bristol Road, the A38. The road leads south to North Petherton. The glory of the village is the lofty (120ft high) decorated tower. The church is 15th century. In medieval days there was a vast Forest of Petherton that extended over the Quantock Hills. Remnants of the old forestlands make an attractive tree mix of green in springtime.

5 miles west of Petherton is Fyne Court Visitor's Centre. At Fyne Court (burnt out in 1898) Andrew Crosse carried out early experiments in electricity.

The hills westward are the Quantocks. The ridge (some 12 miles in length) has its highest point (1260ft) at Wills Neck. The uplands of hard rock offer magnificent walking over bracken and heather and there are splashes of yellow gorse at all seasons. In the deep combes deer roam — they were introduced about 100 years ago and the hunting of them causes controversy.

North Newton (even with the fine Stuart Church) would be unremembered but for the find in 1693. When a house was being demolished a treasure of gold and enamel depicting a boar's head was discovered. It bore an inscription in Anglo-Saxon stating 'Alfred had me made'. It is therefore known as 'Alfred's Jewel' and housed in the Ashmolean Museum, Oxford.

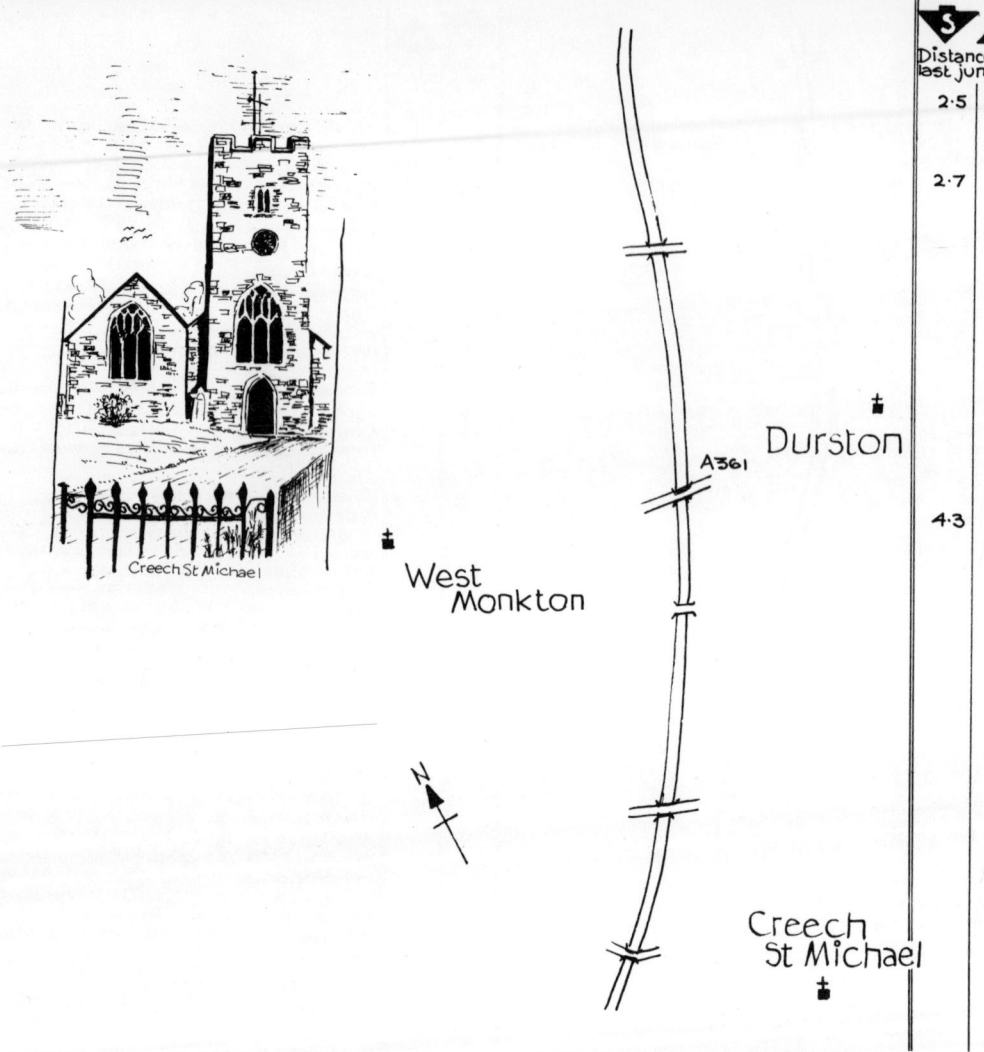

S	N
Distance from last junction	
2.5	4.4
2.7	4.2
4.3	2.6

The soils are now a deep red sandstone but moors are still to the east.

The flatlands are the Curry, Hay and West Sedge moors. The fields were enclosed between 1797 and 1816. New ditches (rhines) were cut as boundaries and the banks lined with willows that provide the basket maker with withies. Vast withy beds were sown in past days. Today they cover about 500 acres and provide about 80% of England's needs. The trade dates from about 1225. The heyday was in Victorian times when basketware was so popular. Today the cut bundles can still be seen drying and weathering by the roadside.

The A361 leads to Street. The skins from the flocks of sheep on the hills were brought to the town for tanning. From this grew the manufacture of sheepskin rugs and gloves. One of the family firms was the Quaker Clark family. Skins that were unsuitable for rugs were made into slippers. With this new expertise the firm started to make shoes. Clarks were to become the largest makers of footwear in the land.

The church at Creech St Michael dates from the 12th century. It is said the two holes in the door are bullet holes!

Distance from last junction	
6.0	.9
6.4	.5
Junction 25	
6.9	6.9

The motor way again passes over the Bridgwater and Taunton Canal (started 1824) that was part of a grandiose scheme to connect Bristol and Devon (with a subsequent exit to the English Channel). This was to bring cheap coal to Devon and to avoid having to sail around the treacherous Lands End.

The River Tone has the same root as many other river names in England - the Thames, Tame Teme etc.

With the great canal scheme Taunton was to be another Liverpool. It was not to be, of course. In medieval times Taunton was a prosperous wool town. The imposing church tower overlooking the town was taken down stone by stone 100 years ago and rebuilt exactly as before. Most of the buildings of the town date from Stuart times - Taunton is today a busy market town and administrative centre.

After the Battle of Sedgmoor Judge Jeffreys journeyed to Taunton to sentence rebel prisoners on the orders of James II - there were 1811 names on his little list! It is said the ghost of the judge walks on September nights - the "Bloody Assize" was in September.

Orchard Portman is only a few scattered farmsteads and a 15th century church.

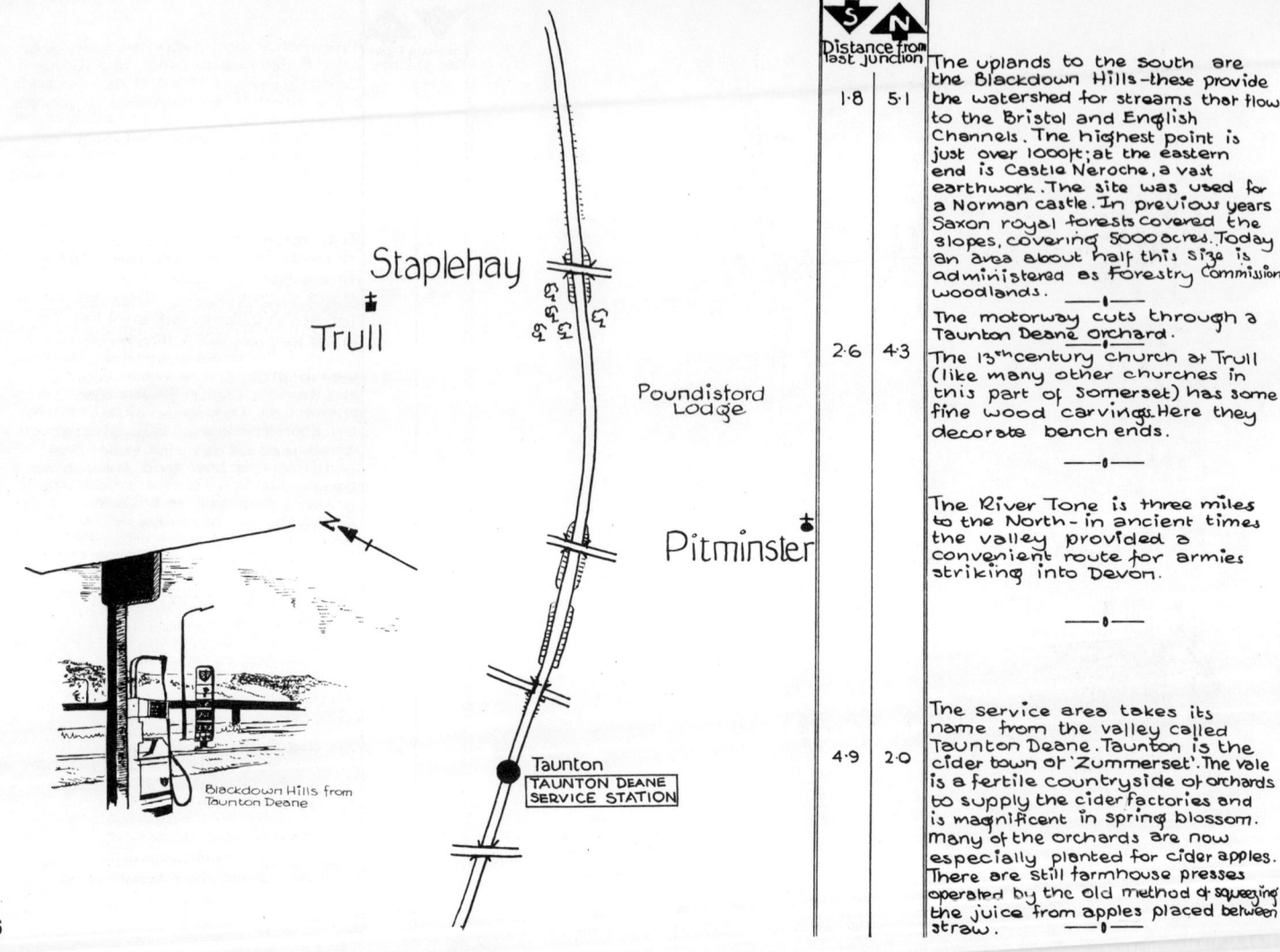

S	N	
Distance from last junction		
1.8	5.1	The uplands to the south are the Blackdown Hills – these provide the watershed for streams that flow to the Bristol and English Channels. The highest point is just over 1000ft; at the eastern end is Castle Neroche, a vast earthwork. The site was used for a Norman castle. In previous years Saxon royal forests covered the slopes, covering 5000 acres. Today an area about half this size is administered as Forestry Commission woodlands.
2.6	4.3	The motorway cuts through a Taunton Deane orchard. The 13th century church at Trull (like many other churches in this part of Somerset) has some fine wood carvings. Here they decorate bench ends.
		The River Tone is three miles to the North – in ancient times the valley provided a convenient route for armies striking into Devon.
4.9	2.0	The service area takes its name from the valley called Taunton Deane. Taunton is the cider town of "Zummerset". The vale is a fertile countryside of orchards to supply the cider factories and is magnificent in spring blossom. Many of the orchards are now especially planted for cider apples. There are still farmhouse presses operated by the old method of squeezing the juice from apples placed between straw.

Blackdown Hills from Taunton Deane

Staplehay
Trull
Poundisford Lodge
Pitminster
Taunton
TAUNTON DEANE SERVICE STATION

St John the Baptist, Wellington

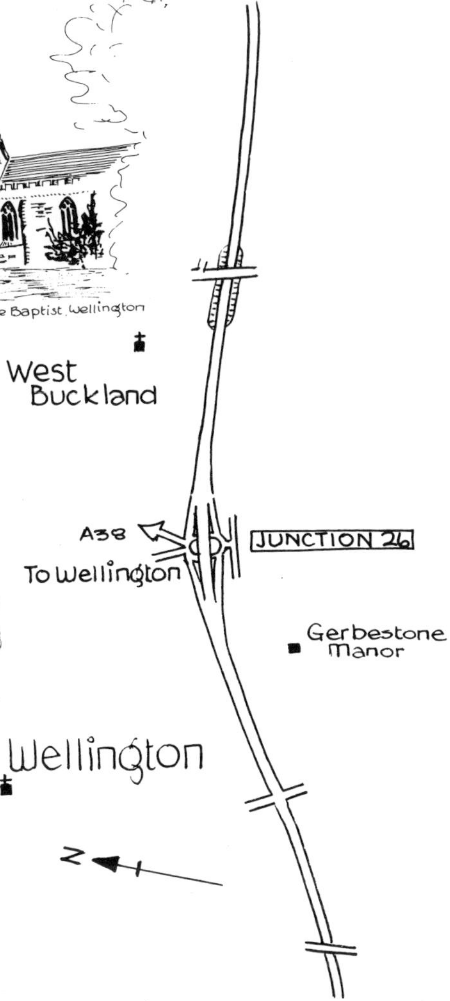

West Buckland

A38 To Wellington — JUNCTION 26

Gerbestone Manor

Wellington

Market Hall, Wellington

Distance from last junction

S	N
6.7	.2
Junction 26	
6.9	8.4
.2	8.2

The tower of West Buckland church is over 500 years old - the church proper is 200 years more ancient. It is situated - like many ancient churches - on the top of a hill so the worshippers could be as close as possible to heaven!

Wellington is the town from which the "Iron Duke" who defeated Napoleon took his title. It was once on the canal but the section westwards after the town was uphill and costly and the waterway perished. There is a small public school founded in the town in the 19th century. For many centuries Wellington has been the centre for the manufacture of serge cloth. The Quaker Were family united the former scattered cottage industry into a large firm that supplied the armed forces with uniform material. It is said the firm received the huge order to provide 1½ million yards of khaki during the first world war — its an ill wind .... etc!

In Wellington's 15th century church is the tomb of Sir John Popham. He was the judge at the trial of Guy Fawkes and also sentenced Sir Walter Raleigh to his death in the tower.

Gerbestone Manor is a fine building from Tudor times.

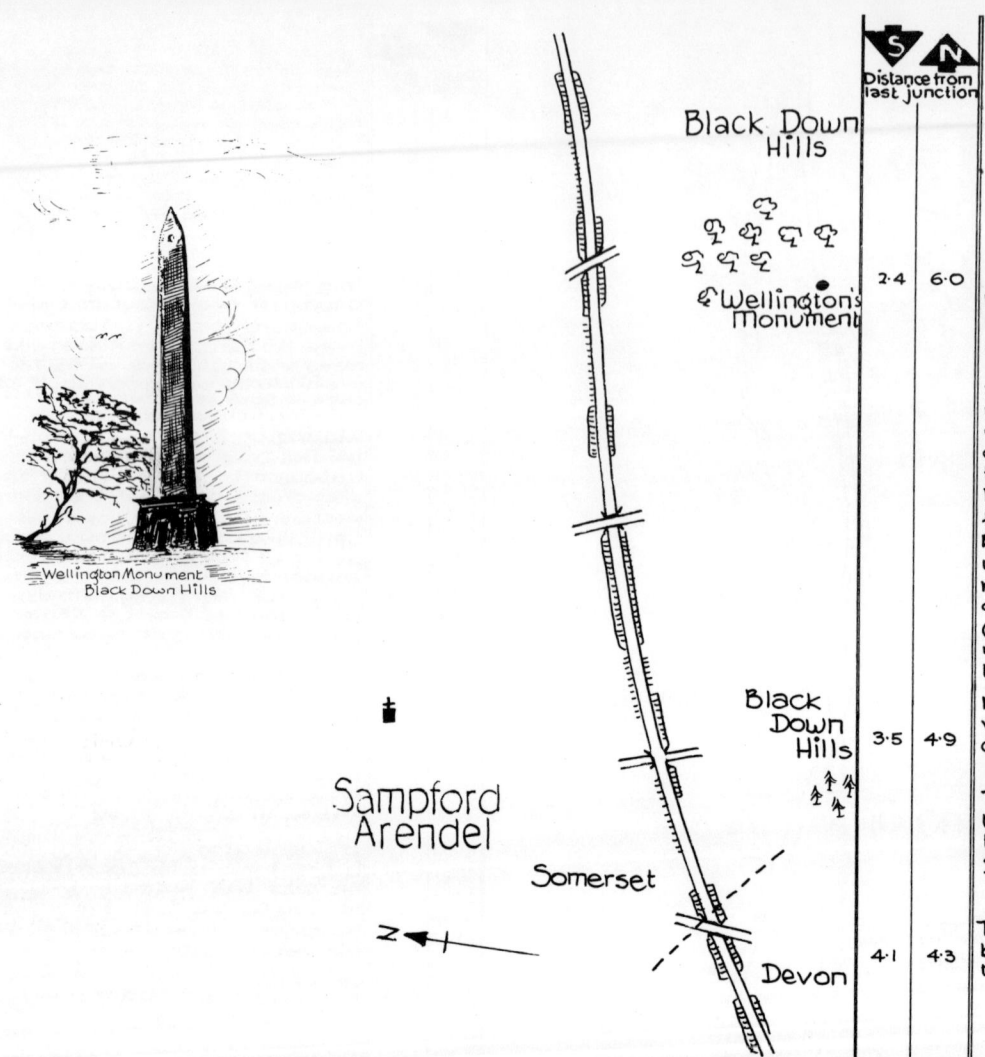

Wellington Monument
Black Down Hills

The reason Wellington chose the Somerset town for the title of his peerage is a little obscure. There was some similarity with his name as he was from the Wellesley family but he never lived or owned property there - but the town felt flattered and soon decided to erect the monument we see - 175ft column on top of the Black Down Hills. The original idea was for the column to be topped by a figure of the Duke; at the base would be cottages for veteran survivors of the Battle of Waterloo. However funds were short and the full scheme never materialised. There are 100s of steps in the tapering obelisk (but no viewing platform!). The monument is now cared for by the National Trust.

Much of the tower of the village church at Sampford Arendal dates from the 13th century.

The M5 now edges nearer to the Black Down Hills - along which the county boundary (Somerset/Devon) runs.

The boundary is now crossed by the motorway (Somerset is to the North, Devon to the South)

48

Ayshford Farm and Chapel by the Grand Western Canal

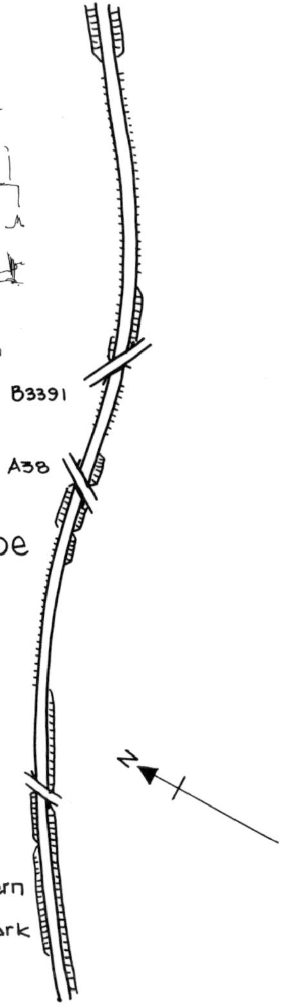

B3391

A38

Burlescombe

Grand Western Canal

Grand Western Canal Country Park

S	N	
Distance from last junction		
		Ten miles away to the north-west are the hills of Exmoor — one of the great National Parks of England and Wales. It rises to its peak (1706ft) at Dunkery Beacon. Much of the moorland is grand and wild and deer and ponies roam. But be warned — it is renowned for having some of the worst weather in Southern England! The moors are associated with "Lorna Doone" for here R.D. Blackmore set his story, basing the plot on local folklore.
6·2	2·2	A few miles along the B3391 is Culmstock. Blackmore lived here as a boy. (His father was vicar). Nearby is an old Quaker Meeting House (founded 1660). In the burial ground famous Quaker names (Rowntree, Cadbury, Fry) appear on simple tombstones.
6·6	1·8	At Burlescombe (in the valley) are the ruins of a Priory that was founded by Maud, Countess of Devon in the 12th century.
7·2	1·2	The former Grand Union Canal is now a unique and fascinating Country Park. The canal meanders and followed the contour line to avoid the use of locks where possible. The waterway was built 1811–14 as a branch of the prospective English/Bristol Channel canal. It is now a fine spread of abandoned and lonely grandeur with a tow-path walk alongside reed and lily-filled pools.

49

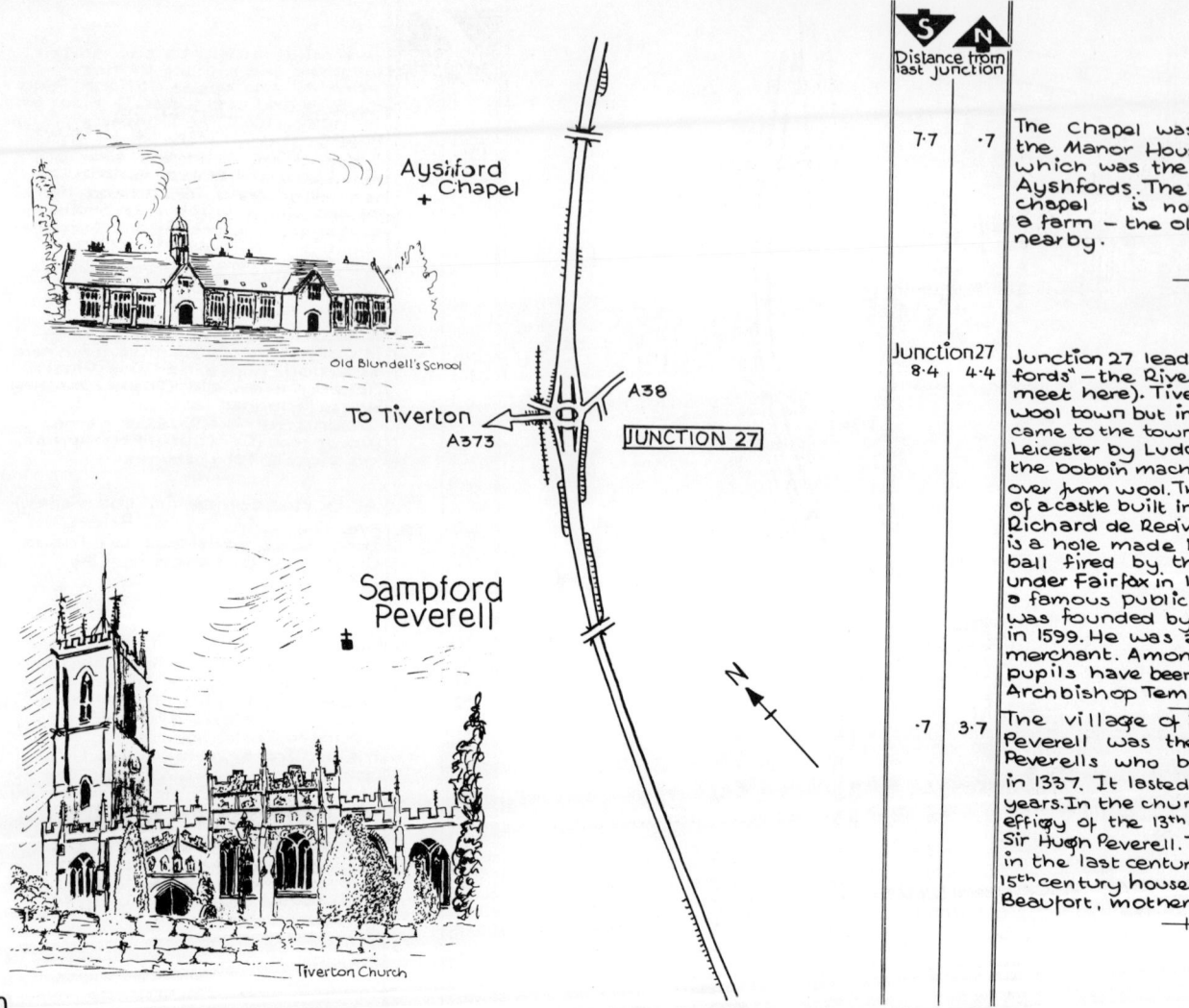

Distance from last junction		
S	N	
7.7	.7	The Chapel was attached to the Manor House of Ayshford which was the home of the Ayshfords. The 15th century chapel is now attached to a farm – the old canal is nearby.
Junction 27 8.4	4.4	Junction 27 leads to Tiverton ("two fords" – the Rivers Exe and Lowman meet here). Tiverton was a wool town but in 1816 John Heathcote came to the town (driven from Leicester by Luddites). He invented the bobbin machine and lace took over from wool. There are remains of a castle built in 1106 built by Richard de Redvers. In the tower is a hole made by a cannon ball fired by the Parliamentarians under Fairfax in 1643. Tiverton has a famous public school. Blundells was founded by Peter Blundell in 1599. He was a wealthy wool merchant. Among the famous pupils have been R.D. Blackmore & Archbishop Temple of Canterbury.
.7	3.7	The village of Sampford Peverell was the home of the Peverells who built a castle in 1337. It lasted for over 400 years. In the church there is an effigy of the 13th century builder Sir Hugh Peverell. The canal makers in the last century took down the 15th century house of Lady Margaret Beaufort, mother of Henry VII.

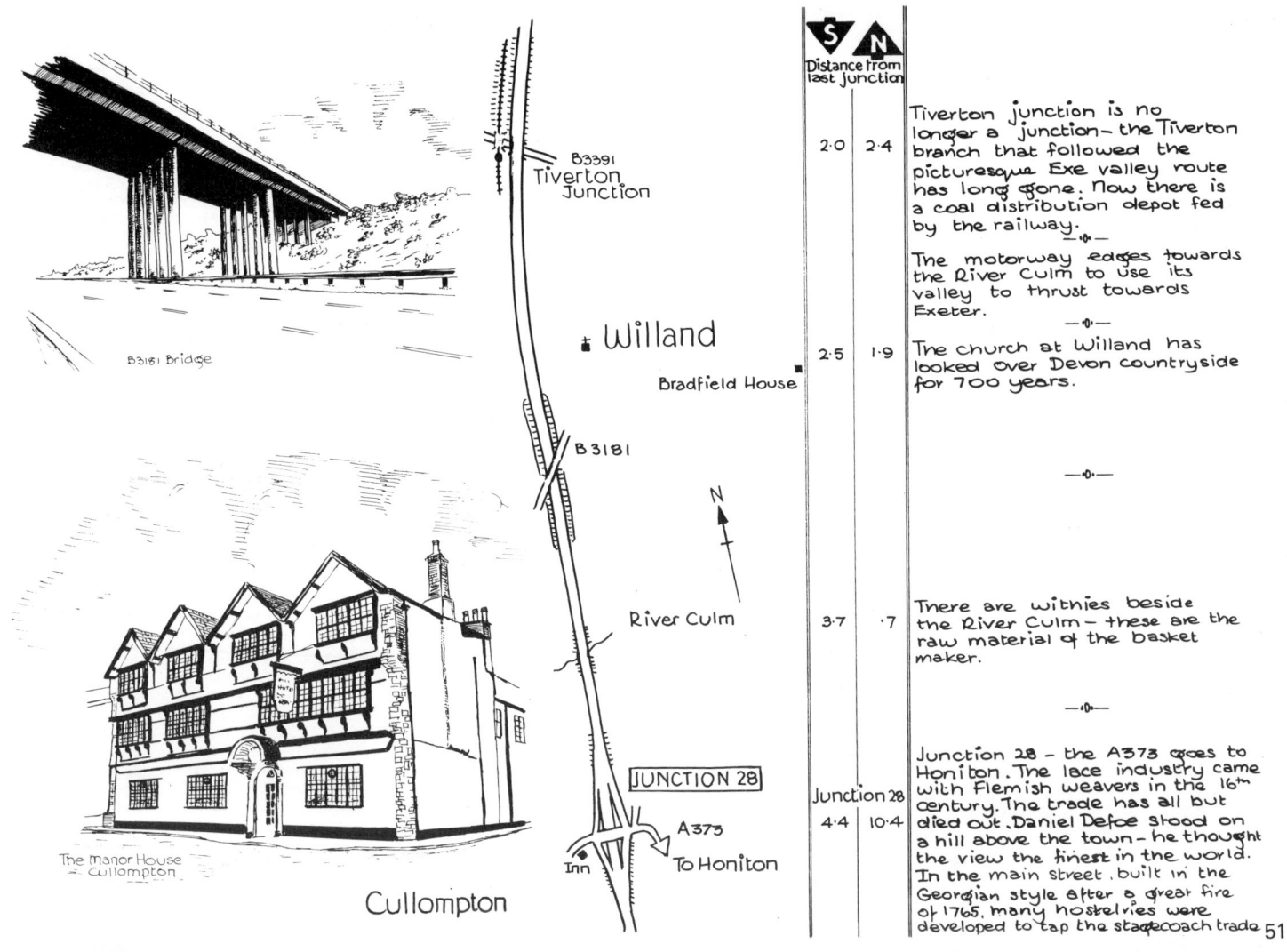

S	N	
Distance from last junction		
2.0	2.4	Tiverton Junction is no longer a junction — the Tiverton branch that followed the picturesque Exe valley route has long gone. Now there is a coal distribution depot fed by the railway.
		The motorway edges towards the River Culm to use its valley to thrust towards Exeter.
2.5	1.9	The church at Willand has looked over Devon countryside for 700 years.
3.7	.7	There are withies beside the River Culm — these are the raw material of the basket maker.
Junction 28 4.4	10.4	Junction 28 — the A373 goes to Honiton. The lace industry came with Flemish weavers in the 16th century. The trade has all but died out. Daniel Defoe stood on a hill above the town — he thought the view the finest in the world. In the main street, built in the Georgian style after a great fire of 1765, many hostelries were developed to tap the stagecoach trade

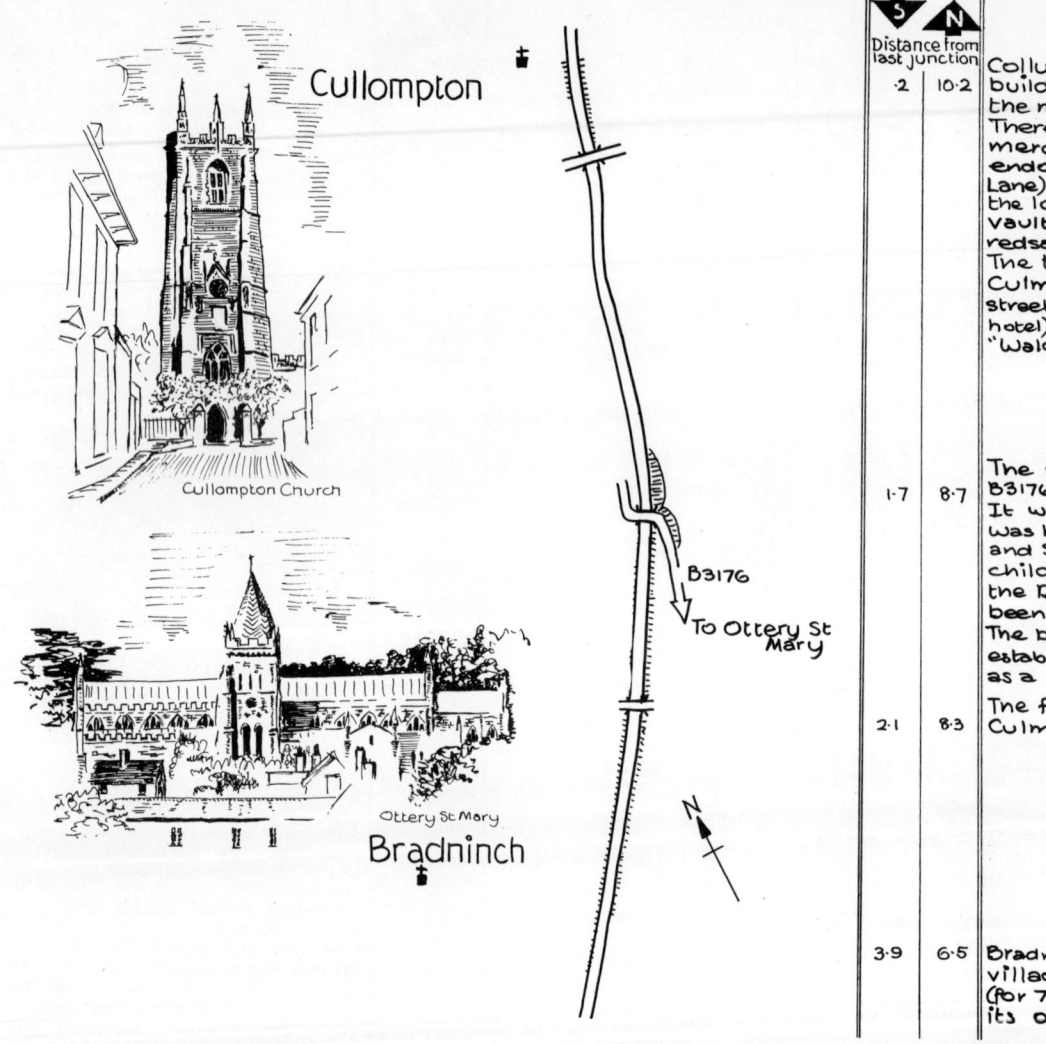

Distance from last junction		
S	N	
.2	10.2	Cullompton has some splendid buildings - the church is perhaps the most interesting in Devon. There were wealthy wood merchants here - they richly endowed the building. One (John Lane) was responsible in 1526 for the lovely South Aisle with its fan vaulted ceiling. The 16th century redsandstone tower rises 100ft. The tributary stream of the River Culm runs each side of the main street. The Manor House (now an hotel) was built in 1603. Nearby is "Waldrons"- a house of similar age.
1.7	8.7	The motorway is crossed by the B3176 that goes to Ottery St Mary. It was here in 1772 that Coleridge was born. His father was vicar and Samuel was the last of 13 children. He wrote a "Sonnet to the River Otter". The church has been called 'a village cathedral.' The building was in 1335 established by Bishop Grandisson as a college for monks.
2.1	8.3	The fertile pastures by the River Culm are rich dairylands.
3.9	6.5	Bradninch.- now a small village below the hills was (for 700 years) a borough with its own mayor.

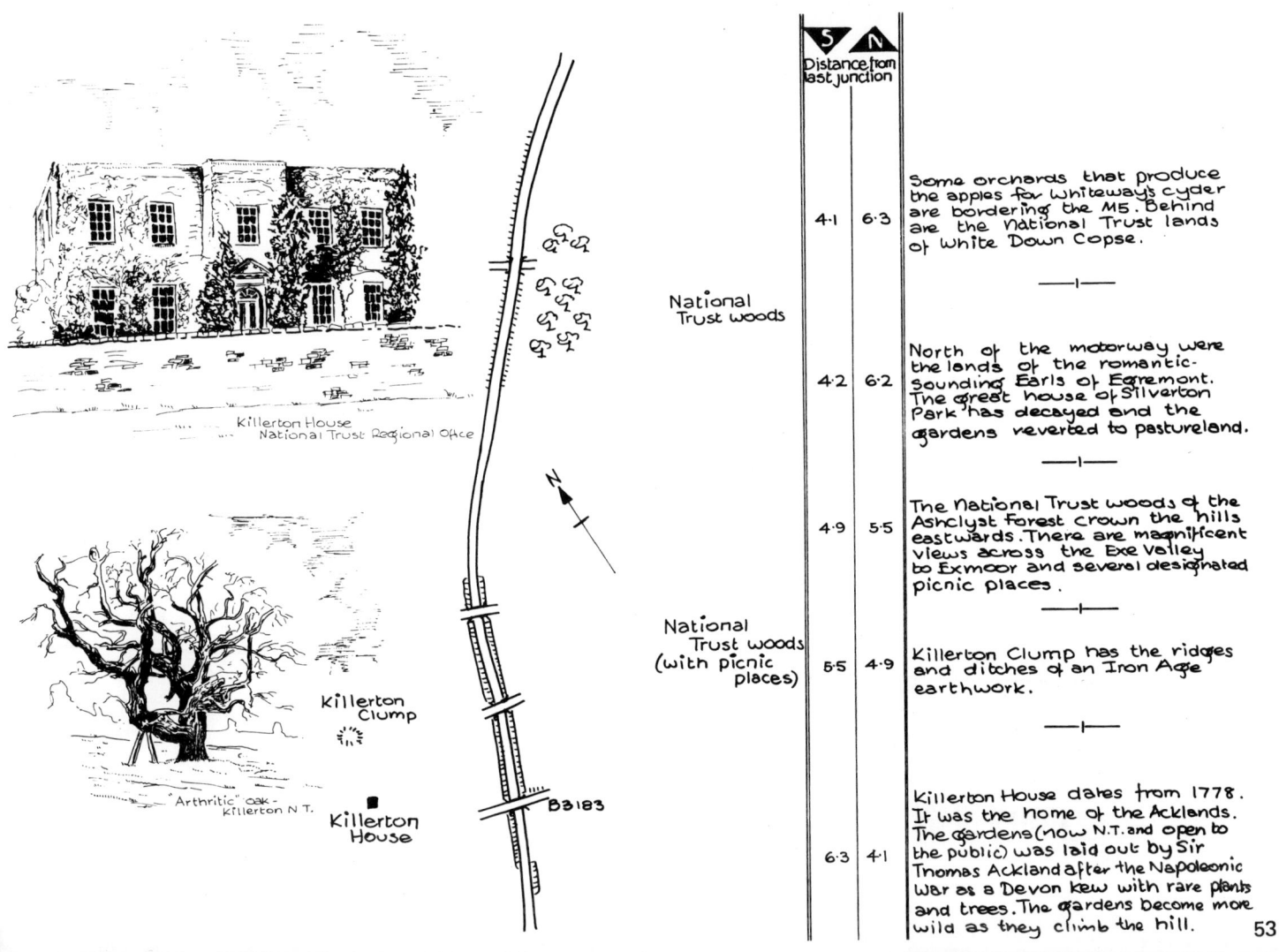

Killerton House
National Trust Regional Office

"Arthritic" Oak - Killerton N.T.

Killerton Clump

Killerton House

B3183

	S Distance from last junction	N	
	4.1	6.3	Some orchards that produce the apples for Whiteway's cyder are bordering the M5. Behind are the National Trust lands of White Down Copse.
National Trust woods	4.2	6.2	North of the motorway were the lands of the romantic-sounding Earls of Egremont. The great house of Silverton Park has decayed and the gardens reverted to pastureland.
	4.9	5.5	The National Trust woods of the Ashclyst Forest crown the hills eastwards. There are magnificent views across the Exe Valley to Exmoor and several designated picnic places.
National Trust woods (with picnic places)	5.5	4.9	Killerton Clump has the ridges and ditches of an Iron Age earthwork.
	6.3	4.1	Killerton House dates from 1778. It was the home of the Acklands. The gardens (now N.T. and open to the public) was laid out by Sir Thomas Ackland after the Napoleonic War as a Devon Kew with rare plants and trees. The gardens become more wild as they climb the hill.

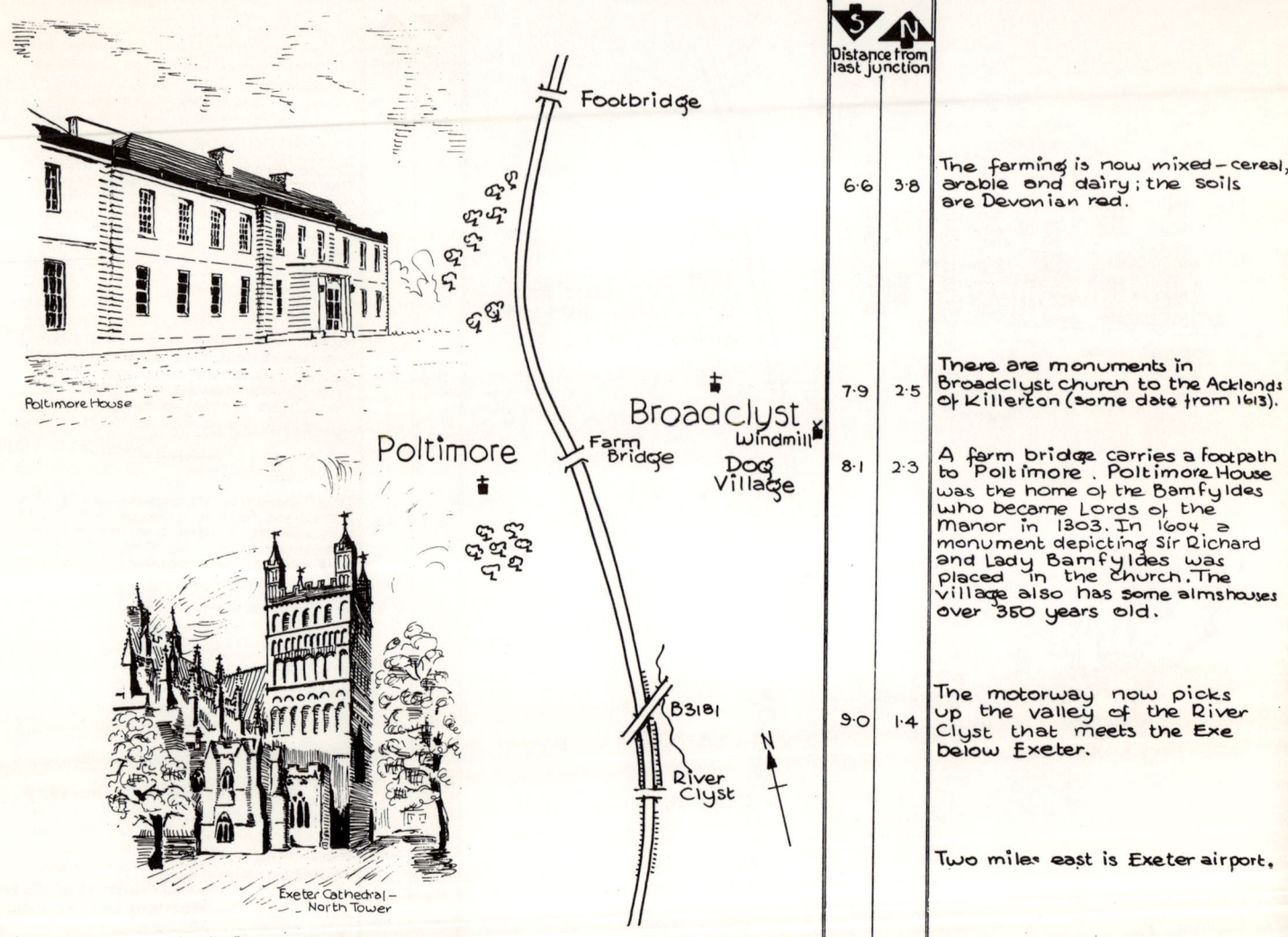

Distance from last junction S	N	
6.6	3.8	The farming is now mixed — cereal, arable and dairy; the soils are Devonian red.
7.9	2.5	There are monuments in Broadclyst church to the Acklands of Killerton (some date from 1613).
8.1	2.3	A farm bridge carries a footpath to Poltimore. Poltimore House was the home of the Bamfyldes who became Lords of the Manor in 1303. In 1604 a monument depicting Sir Richard and Lady Bamfyldes was placed in the church. The village also has some almshouses over 350 years old.
9.0	1.4	The motorway now picks up the valley of the River Clyst that meets the Exe below Exeter.
		Two miles east is Exeter airport.

54

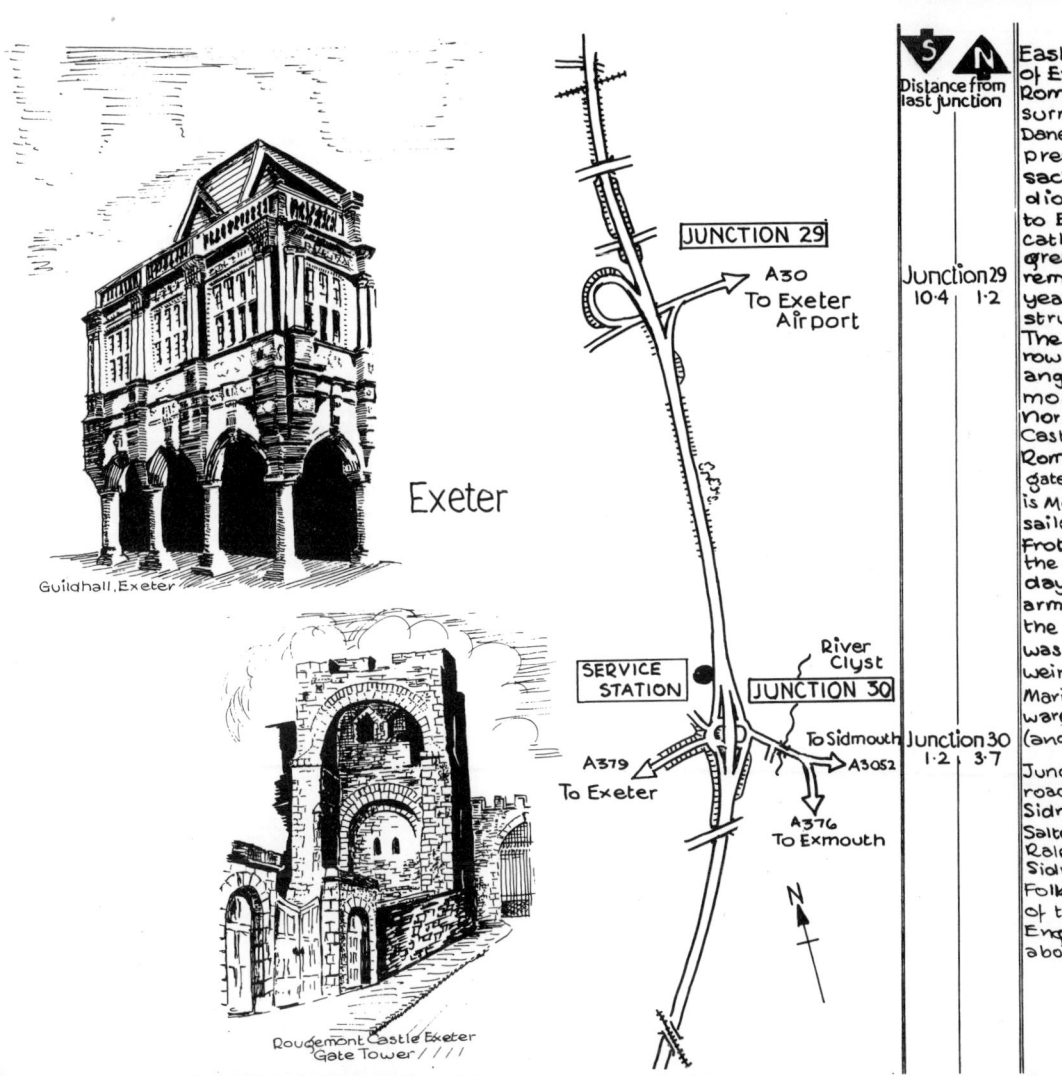

Exeter

Guildhall, Exeter

Rougemont Castle Exeter Gate Tower

JUNCTION 29 → A30 To Exeter Airport

SERVICE STATION

River Clyst

JUNCTION 30 → To Sidmouth, A3052

A379 To Exeter

A376 To Exmouth

Distance from last junction (S / N)

Junction 29 — 10.4 | 1.2

Junction 30 — 1.2 | 3.7

Eastwards is the spread of the city of Exeter – Isca Dumnoriorum to the Romans – who built the protective surrounding wall that withstood the Danes in later years. It could not prevent the Saxon church being sacked in 1003. In 1050 the diocese was moved from Crediton to Exeter. The first Norman cathedral has only the two great towers and nave walls remaining. In the hundred or so years 1256 to 1369 the earlier structure was largely rebuilt. The west front with its three rows of statues of monarchs, angels, clerics etc is perhaps the most beautiful in England. The Normans built their Rougement Castle (perhaps on the site of the Romans' fortress) but only the gatehouse remains. Near the cathedral is Mols Coffee House where sailors like Drake, Hawkins and Frobisher gathered. The Guildhall is the oldest in England (dated from the days of Elizabeth I). She gave the city arms carved and painted to celebrate the Armada's defeat. The Avon waterfront was developed as a port until the weir of 1290. By the Quay is the Maritime Museum in the 19th century warehouses – a great place for boys (and girls) of all ages!

Junction 30 (Information kiosk here) roads lead to lovely seaside places like Sidmouth, Exmouth and Budleigh Salterton. At East Budleigh Sir Walter Raleigh was born. Each August Sidmouth hosts an International Folk Festival. Here also is one of the oldest cricket pitches in England – it was laid about 1800.

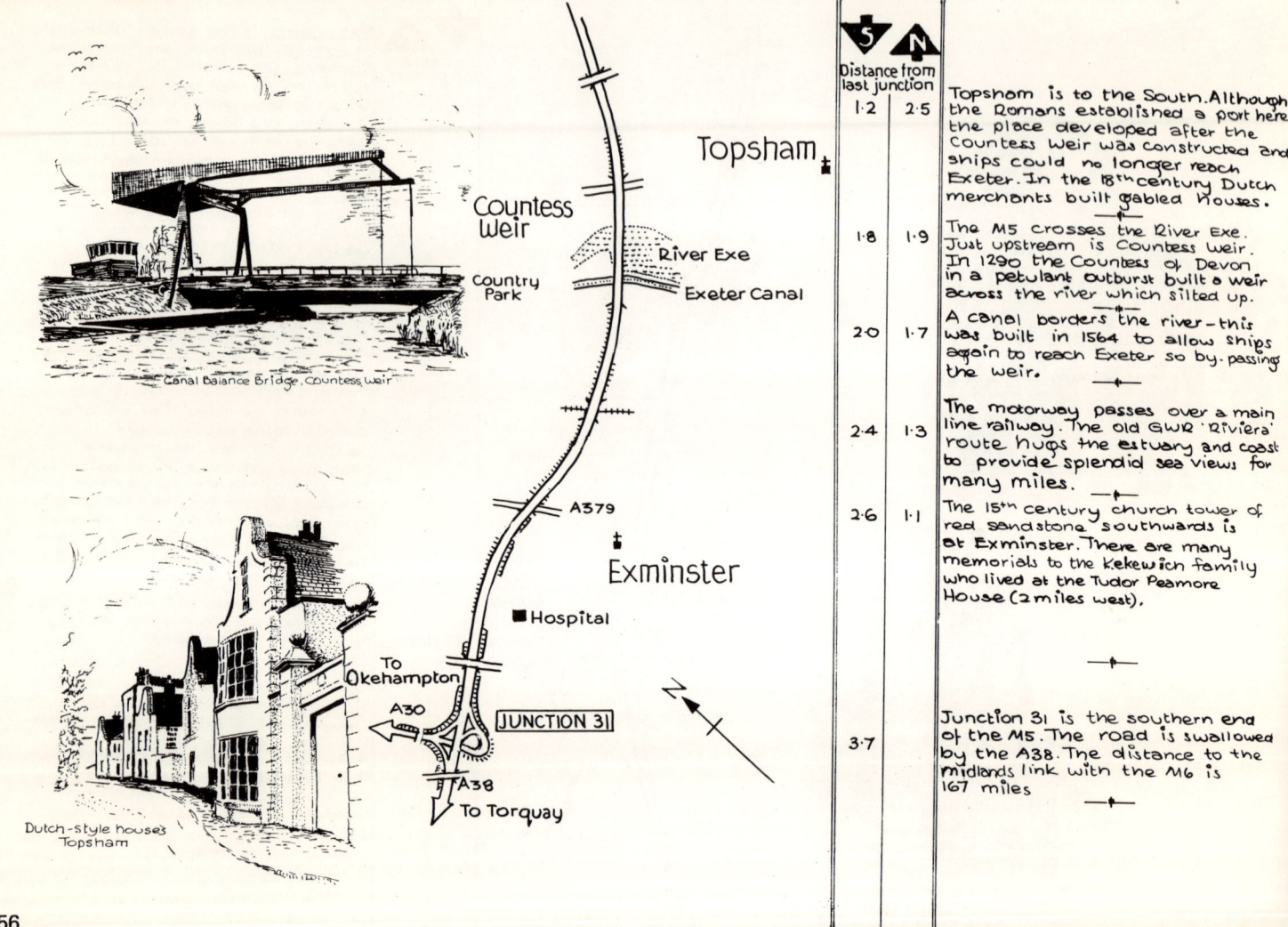